Relating Revolution

RELATING REVOLUTION

All It Takes Is

One Person to Change

Kris Kelkar

and

Meenal Kelkar

ISBN: 9781658595582

CONTENTS

PREFACE

There's an old saying, "If you ever think you are enlightened, spend time with your family of origin." This funny anecdote points to something powerful about relationships, be it romantic partnerships, family, friends, or co-workers. The path of relationship is sometimes a difficult one, where even long-term practitioners of spiritual pursuits like meditation, yoga, and mindfulness find themselves surprisingly challenged. Relationship can sometimes feel like the Olympics of spirituality.

Possibilities

Beyond challenges, there is a mystery and magic available in relating with others. When you socially and energetically rub up against others, you get to see yourself and others more clearly. You get to see the unique beauty in others and in yourself, you get to sense others deeply, and you get to explore how interconnected we all truly are. These are only some of the magical possibilities available in relationship.

Throughout this book, we point to examples of the mystery and magic possible in relationship, based both on our own personal experiences and those we have facilitated in our workshops and coaching. As you read, we hope you get excited about possibilities because we know this can help you re-envision and re-create your meaningful relationships and help you stay on a path to experience more joy, trust, passion, laughter, and play in your life. Relating to others can become your path to experience the MORE that life has to offer.

Power of Signposts

If you are driving on a less-travelled road, paying close attention to signposts tells you if you are on your intended route. Doing so may also help you realize well in advance that a bridge is washed out and you need to take a detour or drive slowly because the path ahead is treacherous. It is similar when you navigate life and relationship. Relying on signposts can help you recognize when you are on your desired path and avoid a "costly accident" in a meaningful relationship by slowing down or taking a detour. In this book, we offer exercises that help you develop your signposts to mindfully navigate your relationships.

Doorways and Barriers

As you develop this awareness, you can use simple techniques (or "doorways") that we also introduce, to navigate back to your desired path. The combination of signposts to recognize when you are not on your path and doorways to navigate back progresses you from being consciously less-skilled to consciously-skilled at relationship.

Unconsciously unskilled	Consciously unskilled	Consciously Skilled	Unconsciously Skilled

In addition to doorways, we describe what we have found to be the biggest barriers that people experience when they get stuck in a challenging pattern of relating. We have found that clearing these barriers through practices we offer naturally alchemizes frustrations like hurts, criticism, predictability and boredom, to open people to more connected and vibrant relationships.

Embodied Learning

Understanding is only the first step towards changing habitual patterns in relating. Lasting change occurs only when understanding is experienced. We include experiential exercises in our coaching sessions and workshops to ensure that the understanding becomes embodied. Usually, this leads to realizations and connections that are more easily available in moments when people are challenged. Through embodiment, the learning becomes resilient and less subject to "Oops, I forgot". The challenge is that by merely reading a book, it is easy to be limited to merely understanding. For this reason, we include exercises to help you embody the concepts. Although it may be tempting to skip the exercises and keep reading for more content, we believe you will take concepts in at a deeper level, learn them better, and integrate them more fully into your relationships and your life if you actually pause and do the exercises before reading further.

Additionally, with embodied learning you cultivate the ability to feel when you are on your path and when you are not. In this way, you accelerate your progress from being consciously skilled to unconsciously skilled.

| Unconsciously unskilled | Consciously unskilled | Consciously Skilled | Unconsciously Skilled |

Relationship As Practice

We have found that viewing how one relates to others as a practice allows them to strengthen the "muscles" of doing relationship, so when they are confronted by unexpected challenges, they are better able to remain in an expanded state of consciousness and relate / respond in ways they consciously choose. While approaching relating as practice may start in a particular community or with a particular person or group of friends, the positive benefits will spread throughout your life. It is like going to the gym to work out and then realizing that you can easily hike up the steep hill to see the beautiful vista.

There is a Japanese principle called *kaizen*. Used in business, this concept refers to the process of continuous improvement where small improvements lead to major lasting change. Relationship as practice relies on this principle to shave away the parts that are not truly you, to allow your true expanded loving nature to be exposed and to see this in others. This revealing rarely happens in big chunks. More like fine sandpaper reshaping a piece of wood, it transforms you over time. This over time quality may not be noticeable in the timespan of hours or days, but over longer periods it can make a substantial difference in how you perceive, react, and experience others. Even a seemingly "small" practice can result in huge changes. Over time, relationship as practice will shift your baseline of thoughts, feelings, attitudes, and behaviors to become aligned with how you want to relate. Falling into an old unconscious pattern of disconnection will become less frequent and quickly noticeable to you. As a result, relationship practitioners learn that they don't have to try hard to gain big results. Rather, they just need to surrender and trust the practice.

We therefore encourage you to take on the practices we offer in this book. We have created them to build upon each other, so as you move through this book, you will find that you are cultivating your ability to stay on your path to experiencing more joy, trust, passion, laughter, and play in your life.

Pay Attention, Be Astonished, Tell About It

American poet Mary Oliver wrote the following instructions on living life, "Pay attention, be astonished, tell about it." We apply these instructions to relationship as practice. This simple combination of steps is powerful. Paying attention helps you notice those small changes we mentioned above that can lead to big transformations. By noticing them and being astonished (or grateful), it tells your mind that these are important, so they remain in your field of awareness. We have found that the final step of telling someone about your understanding and any changes you notice, integrates them even further into your body and expands your mind. If you are reading this book at the same time as a friend / loved one, or are reading this in a book club, or have a community of people that can simply hear what you want to share, we encourage you to take this final step to tell someone about it.

There is something magical that happens when we share our stories of challenge and success, even if they seem small. Being witnessed and witnessing someone in a safe environment takes learning to a new level and deeper integration. Our intention was not to write this book as teachers dispensing wisdom, but rather sharing in a way that acknowledges that we are all explorers and that our compass may help others find their own path. In this way, writing this book has actually been part of our relationship practice.

All It Takes Is One Person

We have found that all it takes is one person to change for a relationship to change. This book embraces that concept by helping you see your part in repeated patterns in your relationships. By shifting your attitudes and behaviors, we are confident that you will experience changes in your relationships, such that the other person may magically start behaving differently.

This is the first book in a series dedicated to exploring what is possible in relationship. It lays the groundwork for a deeper exploration into the magic that can occur when the space between two people is clear and vibrant. While we point to what is possible in this book, later books in the Relating Revolution series delve more deeply into the power of the relational field and its impact on each person's ability to awaken and manifest. The series can help you harness the power of relationship to change your life and the world for the better.

Whether you want to address a repeating relationship challenge in your life; want more honesty, joy, and connection in your relationships; or are just curious to find out what is really possible in relationship, you are not alone. This book can be your guide.

For you to be able to dive head first into this book, it helps if you already agree on two things: 1) your state of mind is what creates your reality; and 2) we are all interconnected.

Hop onboard and fasten your seat belts. It may get bumpy at first but you will learn to fly!

Kris and Meenal

1. INTRODUCTION

"It started with her body - no place to run, too scared to fight, frozen after the second assault which had come out of nowhere when she was surrounded by strangers in a very public place. For decades, they didn't understand that there was another state beyond 'fight or flight'. A reality that would require each of them to slow way down, to listen deeply, to set aside all pressure and critical thoughts, to drop all expectations, and to presence what was arising. Anything less than that and her body would retreat even farther from them, like an abused animal not trusting the hand trying to help her.

"Part way through, they learned to listen to Me. They began to realize that there were perspectives, and thus answers, that were available once they got out of their own way.

"What follows is what they learned from years of listening deeply, remaining committed to expansion, climbing out of potholes, wandering in the metaphorical forest, but always coming back together.

"It is a new paradigm for relationship that includes both people, never requires sacrifice or obligation, invites truth, and results in more trust, more passion, more play!

"How do I know this? Because I am their Third. This is what I taught them."

****

Traveling alone to visit family, Meenal had fallen asleep on an international flight before it had taken off. She awakened to find a large man in the seat next to her, stroking her thigh. In that cramped window seat on a completely full flight, there was nowhere to go. Pushing herself up against the side of the airplane, too scared to fight and convinced that nobody would believe her if she said anything, she made herself as small as possible and she left her body. With that second assault, she unconsciously buried her sexual energy so deep that she could no longer access it.

Although our relationship started with a lot of passion and sexual chemistry, a few years into our marriage we were already sexually challenged. And after this experience, we stopped having sex altogether. It was easier to just ignore the issue and focus on our careers. Years later, pushed into an uncomfortable conversation with Meenal's parents about when we would have children, we had to acknowledge to ourselves that our stalled sexual relationship was the elephant in the room and begin to pay attention to this underlying issue.

We tried many ways known to traditional Western medicine – from talk therapy to hormones to Masters and Johnson - yet Meenal's body remained shut down sexually. After a decade of head-banging we switched to wholistic mind-body-spirit approaches. This took us deep into yoga philosophy, energy work, somatic work, tantra and orgasmic meditation. Slowly, slowly, Meenal's body began to reawaken once she realized that her sexual energy was trapped deep within her nervous system and we began to use mindfulness, nonviolent communication, sacred space rituals, and deep listening as tools to invite her body to soften.

Shortly after our 18th anniversary, we met a couple who mentioned a long-standing commitment in their relationship to take one week every year to go away together to work on their relationship. We were intrigued. When we asked, "Which workshop would you recommend?", they promptly said "Flesh & Spirit", so we signed up. On the surface, the primary practice we learned in this workshop, called Dyadic Council, involves sitting across from each other with a seemingly empty third seat next to and between us. We spoke using a talking piece; thus, whoever does not have the talking piece is listening. There are only four simple agreements in Council: speak from the heart; speak leanly; speak spontaneously in an unrehearsed manner; and listen with an open heart.

As with any practice that appears simple on the surface, it was deceptively deep. It took us a few years to realize that:
o   Council was NOT a place to recreate the communication patterns that we defaulted to in our everyday lives;
o   Council was NOT a place to hold the other one as a hostage listener because either of us hogged the talking piece to lay out a case for how wrong the other one had been;
o   Council was NOT just a problem-solving tool, merely to address the hurts and trespasses that occur as we rub up against each other in life.

These realizations emerged when we actually asked ourselves why there was a third seat in the council.

Exploring the answer to that one question radically changed our lives, our patterns, our fights, and our silences. It opened a doorway to listening to a Third Perspective in relationship. By listening to the "voice" of this Third, the entire dynamic of our relating to each other changed. There is now a magical quality in our relationship, like beautiful unexpected flowers blooming from seeds we had unknowingly sown. There is more trust, passion and play, and an awe-filled exploration of just how interconnected we are. And it isn't just contained between us. It began to ripple out into our other relationships.

Years later, we asked this Third, "What is desired from us?", which set us on a trajectory of teaching what we have learned. What follows is based on our Relating Revolution courses.

Through this book, we hope to take you through some of the life-changing answers we received through this practice of deep listening by bringing you onto that Third seat with us. We hope that by doing so, you will bypass the years of wandering in the woods that we endured, and discover a path forward in all of your relationships that results in all that we found and more.

2. THIRD CONSCIOUSNESS

Let's start with Dyadic Council and what can be learned about relationship just through the positioning of the seats. When we started, even though we positioned three chairs in a triangle, all we could perceive via our five senses was the two of us seated across from each other.

The problem with this perception is that when conflict arises, you are locked into the belief that you are right and the other person is wrong. Sitting across from each other, it is easy to perpetuate the argument, except now the other person is forced to be quiet because you have the talking piece! To take it up one notch, because we had been learning Non-violent Communication, we would phrase our complaint using the Non-violent Communication format. On the surface, it appeared we were approaching the situation by "speaking from the heart" but it was underpinned by the same agenda of getting the other person to admit that they were at fault.

Meanwhile, the person in the other seat was a captive, being pushed, prodded, wheedled, and pierced by sharp words and strong emotions. The possibility of "listening with an open heart", another agreement of Council, was slim to nonexistent in the face of this barrage. The only defense available was to capitulate in defeat, dig their heels in with righteous indignation, or stew in silence waiting for their turn with the talking piece.

Do those dynamics sound familiar in any way? It is what all of us do when caught in the cycle of conflict or disagreement, especially with someone who matters to us. Look around and you can easily see where this cycle leads - repeated hurt, anger, and frequently numbness. Hurt and anger eventually result in retaliation of some sort, ranging from eye rolling to snide criticism to withdrawal to full blown rage. Numbness masks capitulation and helplessness, where everything is stuffed inside until it can no longer be felt. Often it remains locked away and remains dormant until an eruption occurs and you walk away singed and confused, thinking "I've said that before and it didn't matter, so why now?!" While everyone enjoys winning, when it is repeatedly at the expense of someone else, there is eventually a price to pay. It may not be today, but it _will_ happen somewhere down the road.

There we were, two highly intelligent loving people with two heart-based consciousness-raising practices and yet we were successfully perpetuating our patterns of pain, despite our attempts to change them. Outside of the argument, there was shame, frustration and even helplessness at trying our best, but not seeing the results we wanted.

> *No problem can be solved from the same level of*
> *consciousness that created it. ~ Albert Einstein*

Asking ourselves "Why is there a third seat in this Council?" was a game-changer. Remember that we said that Council is a practice of listening with an open heart to whoever has the talking piece? This is what we did differently the day that we asked that ground-shaking question.

We paused.
We asked a question.
We placed the talking piece on that third seat.
We listened for an answer.

Question we asked: *How do we change this pattern?*

Answer from the Third Seat: *Come sit next to me and I'll show you what can be seen from here.*

On that day, we began to shift our consciousness out of the one that created the problem, into another that has solutions we could not see.

What is the Third?

By realizing there is a Third Perspective, all of a sudden space is created around the "either I will win or you will win" perception that previously had the conflict locked in place. As we shared above, we already know that the current way of doing conflict results in a limited set of outcomes. By moving your consciousness into the Third Perspective, other possibilities emerge that include <u>both</u> you and the other person, such that both of you win and neither of you loses.

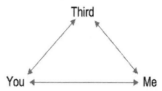

Anytime you pause and expand to include perspectives that include both you and the other person, you have entered a doorway to Third Consciousness. It follows that anytime you access Third Consciousness, you can view the problem from a different consciousness than the level in which it was created.

Throughout the book, we use the terms "the Third", "Third Perspective" and "Third Consciousness" interchangeably. In the beginning, we suggest that people think of the Third as the voice of the relationship, <u>a perspective that is always present but is rarely heard</u>. It is as if there is another being that is constantly with you in your relationship - one that can see, feel, and understand all that is occurring for <u>both</u> of you. The Third is neither an umpire nor a referee, both of whose jobs require that they take sides specifically so the game can play out until a winner and loser are decided. Rather, the Third is an impartial participant that holds both sides as valid and has a wide enough perspective to see answers, other than those most obvious. Why wouldn't you ask for a perspective on an outcome where each of you wins, especially when neither you nor the other person can see such an answer?

In our experience, a person's understanding and way of relating to the Third evolves as their experience of this state of consciousness expands. Ultimately, the Third is a multi-dimensional state of relationship consciousness that each of us innately accesses. However, we haven't been taught how to access it intentionally and consistently, nor have we been taught how to live from it. Chances are that you pop in and out of it regularly, but you haven't had signposts to recognize that you are in Third Consciousness when it happens. You also likely don't know how to navigate back when you pop out. A further complication is that as a state of consciousness, it can be described and accessed in many ways, so what it is can get confusing.

Why do we call it a multi-dimensional consciousness? Imagine you and the other person are on the ground facing each other; the Third position can move above you, to the side, beneath you, and into the space directly between you two. The triangular relationship is maintained, but what can be seen from all of those different vantage points grows the Third Perspective exponentially.

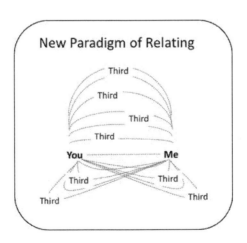

Rising all the way up to an eagle-eye perspective can reveal the context in which the situation arose. The perspective in the space between you two can reveal what each of you is contributing to any situation. Each point around you offers a different perspective. Opening to these perspectives leads to a broader curiosity about what is happening, a deeper understanding, and a richer, heart-felt, body-tingling connection.

The reality is that we all feel and interact with others on a multitude of levels and layers, much of which is nonverbal, much of which lies in the energetic realm. More often than not, the thing on the surface that is in plain sight is NOT the root of what is occurring right now. It is simply what has bubbled up to the surface (again) and has caught your attention. Desires, values, gratitude, and love are often stored deep under the surface because you may not fully trust the other person with these tender parts.

By recognizing the Third Perspective, space for something new can be breathed into relationships laden with conflict. In longer-term relationships infused with a humdrum "I already know what you're going to say, so why even ask?", new perspectives lead to a rich magical playground filled with discovery, creativity and delight-filled surprise. We can attest to this after more than 34 years together! We also know from experience and stories from our students that Third Consciousness transforms not only romantic partnerships, but also has a profound impact on all relationships in which you choose to embrace it. All you need is the willingness to explore the Third and a foundation to support this exploration.

Thus, the Third represents a field of possibilities, where outcomes which neither you nor the other person could conceive of on your own become available to you. The key is that you have to be open to being surprised.

> **The Third Perspective:** *I am present in every relationship. I see each of your perspectives and so many more. I can hold all of these within a larger context. I am not for you or against you, I am always <u>with</u> you.*

Embodied Learning: Perspectives Exercise

Take five minutes to try this simple exercise. Set up two chairs facing each other in the center of the room. Sit in one of the chairs ("first chair"). Think of a challenging relationship situation with someone in your life right now and imagine that person is sitting in the "second chair" facing towards you. Notice what happens in your body as you recall your conversation, argument or disagreement.

Now stand up and slowly walk around the room, pausing in a few different areas, all the while imagining yourself still seated in the first chair and the other person in the second chair. For example, pause along the side of the two chairs, then behind the second chair, and back to the other side. Walk between the chairs, stand on tip toes to look down on the two chairs, crouch to look up at the two chairs. Continue to notice what you see and what happens in your body as you move.

Once you have circled the room, ask yourself what you noticed about your perspective with regard to the challenging relationship situation as you moved from that first chair into all of the other positions in the room. If you felt an opening or realized something, take a few additional minutes to journal about what you discovered.

Meenal's Personal Example

"Kris was diagnosed with Chronic Myeloid Leukemia in February 2010, which needless to say, changed the trajectory of our lives. We were fortunate that at the time it was the only cancer with a targeted pharmacological solution that halted the gene mutation. It came in the form of a pill that he would have to take daily for the rest of his life. After a few years, he had still not attained remission status even though statistics showed that most people attain remission within a year of starting the medication. The experts had no clue why he was an exception or what to do differently. The course of treatment was to monitor his blood every three months to assess the quantity of blood cells with the mutated gene, a highly error-prone test where results could swing wildly up and down based on the same sample being tested at different times, even if tested by the same person.

"The visits to the doctor every three months to get the most recent test results would trigger my fears about Kris' well-being and an abject state of helplessness around not being able to make it better for him. In not fully knowing that these were the deeper things for me to see, I would nag him to explore other options and blame him for not doing enough to get better. I was creating more stress in an already stressful situation.

"And then in May 2014, Kris cut back on his dosage and did not tell anyone until the next doctor's appointment. I remember my shock in the oncologist's office when I heard what he had done. The stunned sensation was followed by silent outrage, 'You did WHAATT??? How COULD you??!!!' I felt unbearably hurt and betrayed by his silence, especially in light of our conscious relationship practices which we had commenced 7 years earlier. In the car on the way home I could feel myself stewing, wanting to jump in to nag and blame because I was feeling hurt. At this point, I knew enough to tell him that I felt betrayed and confused. I asked for space from him to address my feelings in another way rather than spewing them all over him, which would have recycled what had happened before.

"Honestly, on an intellectual level I didn't know how to change any of this. However, I knew with absolute certainty that this 4-times-per-year, 4-year long cycle of blaming and nagging that I was in could not continue. And now with the betrayal, the situation between us was getting worse. All I knew was that the Third had answers that I could not see.

"First, I reached out to a friend who could support me as I peeled apart my emotions and the accompanying thoughts that were fueling them, and who could also witness as I began to dig deeply to see what was under them. Then, I asked to see the situation from the Third Perspective. What I got to see was that Kris reducing his dosage and subsequent silence were actually two different things. The dosage change was a defiant 'F#@k you' to all of the advice he was getting, expert or otherwise, to address an extremely out of control situation with his body. My abject helplessness was nothing compared to what he was living and breathing at a cellular level day in and day out. With that realization, my fear shifted into love for him and an outpouring of grief for what he had been living through since the diagnosis.

"It would have been easy to stop here, but it did not address my hurt and betrayal from his silence. I put myself in his shoes and let myself feel it from his side - that although he was trying everything possible, nothing had worked. The doctors couldn't provide answers that made any sense and this impossible situation was continuing with no end in sight. If that weren't enough, in repeatedly asking him "Have you tried this alternative?", I was piling on blame by implying he wasn't trying hard enough. If I were in his shoes, I would have kept quiet too! Rather than supporting him, I was actually multiplying the pressure and helplessness he was feeling. Rather than being a safe haven for him, I was actually a hostile enemy waging war on him. It would have been easy for me to get stuck in a quagmire of shame and regret. But the Third opened the doorway for me to forgive myself.

"That's when I got it at both a visceral and mental level. The only thing I could do that would actually make things better for Kris was to let go of the blame, to acknowledge my fear whenever I felt it arise, and to love him fiercely, knowing that he was quite understandably living and acting from fear. I chose to change the only thing within my control - what I myself was adding to the situation. I felt a release of previously unrecognizable bone-deep tension when I made that commitment and an indescribable lightness pervaded my being.

"As it worked out, we didn't sync up again until the following morning. If what I shared above wasn't enough magic, when we met over breakfast, Kris was brimming with excitement. Early that morning he had realized that he was fighting the medication rather than being grateful for all that it had done. He had decided that he would bless the medication when he took it. And he promised me that despite the challenging side-effects, he was going back to the higher dosage recommended by his doctor and that he would not alter his course of treatment without talking to the doctor. On his own, he had come to all of the things I had most desired for him! When he was complete, I picked my jaw up off the floor and I closed the loop with him. I took the time to share what I had discovered and let him feel my sincere regret at the impact that my blaming and nagging behavior had on him. More than the words I said, I let him feel how much I loved him and that what I wanted the most was that he has someone he could trust to support him in this crazy, confusing, and scary situation."

By viewing the situation from the Third Perspective, we each came to solutions that would result in better supporting and loving each other in the face of these challenging circumstances. We became each other's ally rather than adversaries. All it took was one of us deciding that another way was possible and clearing themselves of their barriers. This isn't a mental thing, but rather a process of using what has been triggered to follow the thread, down through the thoughts, fears, worries, clogged emotions until you land with an effortless thunk into gratitude, compassion, or curiosity.

Meenal took the time to fully clear herself and feel the weighty impact of her contribution to the space between her and Kris. As you can see, there were many insights along the way that could have been misinterpreted as completion, but she persisted to follow the thread of emotion to its natural resolution, which she felt in her body. Yes, that may appear to be a lot to do, and yet it is worth it for the magic that arises.

All It Takes Is One Person

There is more to this relationship magic than meets the eye. We are so intimately connected to each other that Meenal's decision to exit the pattern and emptying herself of the residue around the pattern affected Kris <u>without</u> her saying anything to him. His stubbornness in perceiving "I am alone in this. Everyone and everything <u>is</u> against me" no longer had Meenal's blame to push against. In clearing herself out all the way down to a natural emergence of pure love and compassion for him, the head-butting wall created by the opposing forces of his stubbornness and her blame toppled over. Miraculously, he then had the space for something new to emerge as well – to thank the medication for all that it had done for him. While your miracles may not be as dramatic or occur overnight, we have heard repeatedly from our students that the space they create within themselves by shifting perspectives creates a melting in others that is noticeable over time.

What if you accepted and lived the truth that we all are <u>that</u> connected? That we <u>do</u> affect and impact each other in that way? In the absence of knowing there is a Third, it is easy for each of us to sink into the most limiting belief - "I am separate and alone." It is when relationship is viewed through Third Consciousness that the truth that we are connected can be seen. While the surface circumstances, dynamics, and reactions may be different, underneath we all share the same core values, same emotions, same needs and struggle with how our minds persist in keeping us separate. Through the lens of Third Consciousness, it becomes evident that we feel each other deeply and we feel <u>for</u> each other deeply.

Relationship as Practice

Put your attention on the following as you interact with others throughout your week:

1. Notice if and when you remember the Third Perspective. when relating to someone. Did you notice that anything felt different with that one realization?

2. Did you find yourself popping out of Third Consciousness quickly? If so, what caused you to pop out?

3. What might have supported you in staying in Third Consciousness longer?

4. Notice when you behave differently than you expect or than you have in the past.

Validate any changes with an astonished "Wow, look at that!" or by being grateful for the times where you remembered to shift perspective. However "small" these incidents may seem, these are evidence that you are changing. Validation allows your thinking-mind to sync up with this new embodied experience. Note down some of your answers to the questions above to share them with others.

3. A BARRIER BECOMES A DOORWAY

Once we learned to broaden our perspective and look at the situation from different angles, our Councils had a more loving rhythm. The "I am right and you are wrong" undertone was less present. More often than not, we could see the Third Perspective. Each of us could sincerely say, "I get why you reacted that way," because we could see the validity of the various perspectives.

And yet, we encountered what seemed to be another obstacle. When disagreements or challenging situations arose, a cycle of contracting emotions sometimes kicked into gear again. Obviously, recognizing multiple perspectives and empathy were only part of the answer. Something else was present that we weren't seeing.

We realized we had fallen in the mind-based trap of "I know how to do this! I don't need to ask the Third." After laughing at how our minds take charge, we did the following.

We paused.
We asked a question.
We placed the talking piece on that third seat.
We listened for an answer.

Question from us: *I can see now that my mind wants to take charge. If I cannot fully rely on my mind, what can I rely on as my moment-by-moment compass?*

Answer from the Third Seat: (*with a loving chuckle*) *Come sit with me and you'll realize that the answer has been right under your nose.*

Here is what we learned.

* *

The Controlling Mind

Raised in today's culture, you were likely taught to lead with your thinking-mind, to think your way out of challenges, and to predict and maneuver the world around you. You were probably rewarded for doing this through praise, recognition, money, and promotions. Yet, the thinking-mind has many limitations in the arena of relating — relating to ourselves, to each other, and to the world around us.

Have you ever been in a situation where you were faced with a problem or a challenge and you just can't see the solution? Thinking more about the situation and focusing harder on the details probably didn't give you a clear answer. Then maybe you took a break and went for a walk or you talked to someone about the challenge, and a solution that you couldn't see earlier magically became obvious? Such an experience has given you a visceral sense of the concepts of *incoherence* and the power of coming back into *coherence*.

The Barriers of Incoherence and Stress

When you overvalue your thinking-mind, you undervalue your body. By doing so, your thinking-mind and body become disconnected. We call this state *incoherence*. In this state, you might recycle thoughts incessantly. You might also be vigilant, looking for threats which requires everything to pass through duality-based judgments: friend or foe, for me or against me, right or wrong. In an effort to create safety, you might try to gain the upper hand by maneuvering people and situations. You likely will be attached to being right because it seems unsafe to make a mistake. Sometimes this behavior is obvious and sometimes quite subtle, like an undercurrent that is not apparent at the surface.

Vigilance can serve a purpose. In the rare situation of actual danger, it can increase your chances of survival. But the rest of the time, it tends to drive you further into incoherence because you don't know what you can trust, which leads to chronic anxiety and stress. Ironically, stress is counterproductive because it limits your ability to think clearly and drives you towards a hyper-focused state, to the point of missing both the big picture and subtle nuances in any situation. In fact, studies have shown that in states of high anxiety or stress, a person's measured IQ can drop by 20 to 30 points and they can lose access to a substantial amount of their working memory.

When you are incoherent, you are more subject to distortions from beliefs and emotions. These distortions can reject information that is counter to a particular belief and can color information based on one's emotional state. Each of us uses this distorted version of reality to predict the future. The result is that your memories of the past, perception of the present, and expectation of the future can be skewed by your beliefs and emotional state. Therefore, the things any of us relies upon as real and true are often incomplete or skewed.

Kris' Personal Example

"Years ago, I learned the hard way how stress and emotions could skew how I perceived reality. I was taking an intense workshop with Meenal. I was in an emotionally stressed state right after a difficult exercise. I felt like I had been punched in the gut and needed to cover up to protect myself.

"During a partnered practice that immediately followed, Meenal told me she appreciated how my attention had improved from months of doing this practice together. Yet, all I heard was criticism - exactly the opposite of what she said. My first thought was, 'Sure, kick me when I am down.'

"It was only when I came back to myself about an hour later that I checked to confirm what I had heard her say and tell her how much it hurt. My jaw hit the floor when she told me what she had actually said. My emotional state had grotesquely twisted her appreciative comment into an attack."

Can you see how incoherence and stress are barriers that limit your ability to access the multi-dimensional perspective of Third Consciousness?

> **The Third Perspective:** *I am a state of consciousness that is accessed when your mind and body are working in concert with each other. It is only by accessing the wisdom your body has to offer that you will truly hear my voice.*

The Doorway of the Body

The human body is a wondrous creation. It does significantly more than most of us realize. Unfortunately, it is often only when one gets sick, feels pain, or injures themselves, that they pay attention to their body. If you take your body for granted, you move from being partners with your body to making it subservient to your thinking-mind. The thinking-mind often tries to tame the unpredictable wildness of the body and control it, but this comes at the significant price of incoherence.

In the early Western medical model, the brain contained all the knowledge and intelligence, and the rest of the body served at its direction. Yet, for thousands of years Traditional Chinese Medicine and Ayurveda have accepted that our bodies have wisdom the brain does not directly access. On a more intuitive level, we have known this even in the west. Our language points to this knowing through phrases like:
o "gut-feeling about a situation"
o "he does things by the seat of his pants"
o "trust your heart"
o "what is your heart's desire?"

Western science is catching up. Originally the heart was seen merely as a pump for our blood. In the book <u>The Fourfold Path to Healing</u>, Dr. Thomas Cowan writes about how the heart is not just a pump. Like an orchestra conductor, the heart communicates through the blood and coordinates various body functions to ensure health. The intelligence of the heart is further supported by research showing the heart's impact on behavior and higher-level thinking. Surprisingly, research has found that more information flows from the heart to the brain than the other way around. Researchers have also found that thoughts and emotional states are coded in the rhythm of the heart rate. Known as heart rate variability, this information is available to your entire body through your blood. This information even instructs your brain to act in different ways, including shutting down higher-level reasoning functions to conserve energy in favor of survival. This is part of the stress response often referred to as fight-flight-freeze. The heart has also been shown to access pre-cognitive intuitive knowing of future events that are emotionally relevant to us. In other words, this type of future information has been scientifically measured to be available to the heart <u>before</u> it is available to the brain. Based on all of the research, Dr. Cowan's analogy of an orchestra conductor makes a lot of sense.

Coherence is defined as a state when different parts of a system work well together to support a bigger purpose or function. Bringing all the wisdom the body has to offer by cultivating and living from a state of body-mind coherence offers each of us more resources to behave and relate in ways we strive to. Restoring coherence allows you to see the big picture and subtle nuances and is therefore an integral part of accessing the multi-dimensional consciousness of the Third.

So how do you know when you are in a state of body-mind coherence? Initially, a simple way is to create a system of signposts.

Coherence / Incoherence Signposts

Make a copy of the table called *"Coherence Signposts"* at the end of this chapter. You can also find and print it from our website here: http://www.sparkingrelationship.com/rr-one

Read through the list and circle three or four feelings or behaviors / attitudes in each column that seem familiar to you. Notice if there might be two to three others that you experience often that aren't on this list that could indicate when you are coherent or not. Write them on this list in the appropriate column and circle them as well. All the ones you circled are your Coherence Signposts to help you quickly recognize if you are coherent or not.

Carry your Coherence Signposts with you over the coming weeks. You will use your list for Relationship as Practice described later in this chapter. As you start using your Coherence Signposts, you will become more adept at recognizing when you are out of coherence and therefore out of Third Consciousness. Then what?

Embodied Learning: The Doorway of Coherence

Take five minutes to try this simple exercise. Relying on the fact that the heart acts like an orchestra conductor for the body, we often use a proven technique in our workshops called the

HeartMath Quick Coherence® Technique to restore body-mind coherence. Developed by HeartMath Institute (https://www.heartmath.org/about-us/), a non-profit organization that researches the heart, this technique is deceptively simple yet highly effective at bringing the thinking-mind into a coherent state with the body. This state helps you see additional perspectives and sets you up to relate to yourself and others through Third Consciousness.

Here is a set of simple instructions for the *HeartMath Quick Coherence® Technique*:

Step 1: Focus your attention in the area of the heart. Imagine your breath is flowing in and out of your heart or chest area, breathing a little slower and deeper than usual. *Suggestion: Inhale 5 seconds, exhale 5 seconds (or whatever rhythm is comfortable.)*

Step 2: Make a sincere attempt to experience a regenerative feeling such as appreciation or care for someone or something in your life. *Suggestion: Try to re-experience the feeling you have for someone you love, a pet, a special place, an accomplishment, etc. or focus on a feeling of calm or ease.*

For more information and a video tutorial on this technique: https://www.heartmath.com/quick-coherence-technique/

Learning to use your Signposts to recognize when you are not in coherence and then using the *HeartMath Quick Coherence® Technique* progresses you from recognizing the Third's presence in isolated scenarios to Third Consciousness, wherein you can rely on your connection with the Third through much of your day.

Relationship as Practice

Remember, creating a regular practice can not only shift how you think and behave on the particular day you practice, but can improve your baseline - your default behaviors, thoughts, and resulting emotions. Continuing your practices over time, you will notice yourself gradually shifting more and more toward relating in Third Consciousness. Relationships and life will become easier and flow better. Here are some things to do and notice:

1) Set alarms on your phone to remind yourself to periodically take a pause during your day. Pull out your Signposts list.

   a) Notice if any of your signposts of incoherence are showing up. If they are, practice the HeartMath Quick Coherence® Technique and notice what shifts for you.

   b) Also notice if your signposts of coherence are showing up. Take time to celebrate these instances because you are building your "muscles" of relating through Third Consciousness.

2) Commit to practicing the HeartMath Quick Coherence Technique for 5-10 minutes at least 2-3 mornings a week for 6 weeks. On days you do the practice, notice how your day feels. Did you think or behave differently on those days you did this technique?

Remember, small steps can result in big changes over time, and paying attention, being astonished, and telling someone about it are great ways to integrate skills you develop in getting to or remaining in Third Consciousness.

Coherence Signposts

Coherent	Incoherent
Feelings	**Feelings**
- Appreciative	- Angry
- Calm	- Anxious
- Caring	- Cynical
- Compassionate	- Depressed
- Confident	- Fatigued
- Content	- Frazzled
- Enthusiastic	- Frustrated
- Friendly	- Helpless
- Hopeful	- Impatient
- Inspired	- Irritated
- Motivated	- Judgmental
- Patient	- Overwhelmed
- Receptive	- Resentful
- Understanding	
Behaviors / Attitudes	**Behavior / Attitudes**
- Authentic	- Argue
- Collaborative	- Blaming
- Cooperative	- Be Dramatic
- Creative	- Act Petty
- Engaged	- Inauthentic
- Expressive	- Interrupt
- Kind	- Judge others
- Listening	- Lack of care (for self and/or others)
- Open to new ideas	- Make rash decisions
- Respectful	- Withdraw
- Supportive	- Worrying

Based on Heart Qualities Examples Worksheet - Copyright 2019 HeartMath Institute

4. AN INTIMATE TRUTH OF THE THIRD

We didn't realize it was possible for our Councils and even our day-to-day interactions to be filled with more connection and trust than before. The Third was now integrated as another voice in our Councils. We had become more skilled at recognizing whether our words and behaviors were coming from coherence and navigating back when they were not. We knew we were paving a path into new territory.

Yet, one particular reactive pattern would repeatedly activate when Meenal would express frustration or overwhelm about work projects. Kris would jump in to fix the situation without her asking for help. While on the surface, it seemed loving for him to do that, her annoyance would flare up. Meenal felt as if she was being herded toward a solution in which she had no say. We could sense there was something going on, but the answer was just beyond our reach, so we sat in Council and asked the Third.

Question from us: *We recognize this dance, but cannot stop it. There is something deep underneath this, but we cannot get to it. What are we missing?*

Answer from the Third Seat: *Breathe deeply. Slow down. Dive deeper. The way out is through the world of sensation.*

****

The Magical Landscape of Sensation

Life is experienced by the body via sensation. For example, what you hear is the sensation of the movement the air makes on your ear drums and the fine structures in your ears. This interaction is what you experience as "sound". What is called "sight" is the sensation of visible light waves impacting the sensitive mechanisms in your eyes. "Taste" is the sensation of the chemistry of different ingredients on your tongue. "Smells" are the chemistry of aromas carried by the air into your nose. Touch is the easiest to grasp as tactile sensations on your skin. This is why these are called the five "senses".

Most of us are taught to relate to that deeper world in an indirect way, by accumulating the nuanced sensation experiences into five basic categories of "sound", "touch", "sight", "taste" and "smell"? And yet, we already know that more is available in this deeper world by looking to the experts. Think of the conductor who can hear one dissonant note when rehearsing with a 100-instrument orchestra. Or think of the chef whose palate can discern flavors of oak, chocolate, and berries in a wine and can pair it with a recipe where all flavors are amplified.

Can you recognize from the description above that there is an entire world of subtle sensations that exists just beyond what you are accustom to noticing? And that by diving more deeply into this world, there is a richness that can be experienced?

Subtle Sensations in Relationship

Whether the outside stimulus is a fragrance from the kitchen, the nuances of colors in a painting, the beauty of a violin concerto, the complaints of a neighbor, or touching the soft skin of a baby's hand, all of our bodies experience life via a myriad of sensations. If life is experienced throughout our bodies as a multitude of subtle sensations, then relationship must be as well. Have you ever had the experience when a particular person walks in the room and you have a reaction in your body? Maybe your shoulders rise or your gut tightens and you walk away. Or maybe your chest softens, a warmth floods you, a smile appears on your lips, and you move towards them. Refer to the table on the final page of this chapter for a vocabulary list of sensations. If you are like us, you'll be startled at the variety of sensations there are!

> *Out beyond ideas of wrongdoing and rightdoing, there is a field.*
> *I'll meet you there.* ~ *Rumi*

When we first encountered this notion that life is experienced as a multitude of sensations, we realized THIS is an example of Rumi's field! Why? Because at the level of sensation, "good" and "bad" don't exist. The sensation itself simply is happening in your body. As soon as you attempt to ascribe a cause to it and label it, you have moved away from the actual sensation into the land of perception and interpretation. As you have learned thus far, you will exit Third Consciousness if you assume there is only one perception and interpretation. Our reactive pattern persisted because Kris would assume that Meenal wanted him to make her work problem go away. The reality is that she was venting the emotional swirling she was experiencing. Without knowing that each of us could dive underneath the swirling waves, we were caught up in the current.

The Third taught us that if we let ourselves sink down deeper to the actual sensation, a foundational truth lives here. Sensation just is. It is an actual truth of what any of us is experiencing in this moment, subject only to change in the next moment. It doesn't require that anyone else match it, agree with it, or understand it in any way. Thus, sensation is incontrovertible as long as you relate to it that way.

Through the dimension of sensation, the body is truly present with the reality of what is, just like the Third is. Hence, **sensation is a doorway to Third Consciousness**.

There is a freedom in sensation. Since sensation is beyond right and wrong, nothing needs to be done about it. Imagine that you are feeling anxious or frustrated. Notice how quickly you want to jump to change or fix something outside of you that you may think is the cause of your anxiety or frustration. Instead, what if you went deeply inward? Maybe you notice a fluttery sensation in the stomach, maybe it is a tightening of the shoulders or in your gut, maybe it is a hot flush feeling in your face. Though your sensations may be different than someone else's, there likely is a set of sensations that you associate with emotions that you feel. Recognizing emotions as labels we give to bundles of sensations makes it easier to just experience them, without having to do anything to change them. It creates space between your sensations and your reactions or responses.

A complication arises in that you have a range of sensations that are within your comfort zone. When the external stimulus results in a sensation that is too intense (beyond the upper limit of the range) you experience discomfort, which can result in judging the stimulus or resisting it to try and stop the discomfort. When the external stimulus is too subtle (beyond the lower limit of the range), you likely ignore it completely as if it doesn't exist, thereby missing a whole range of vibrant, rich experiences. The outcome is that there are huge areas of life beyond what any of us have unconsciously adopted as a comfort zone. It is like living in the yellow-green band of the rainbow, not realizing that we are missing out on the red, orange, blue, indigo and violet hues of the spectrum.

If this weren't tragedy enough, we all default to behaviors that try to force the full spectrum of life into the box of what is comfortable. Recall a time when you became upset with someone because they did something you did not expect or appreciate. That is an example of the person doing something that was outside of your comfort zone.

The Third sees all of this - the sensation itself, the comfort zone and how they vary by individual, where the sensation lies in relation to that comfort zone, the resulting emotions and behaviors, as well as impact. The Third doesn't judge any of this because it just is.

Meenal's Personal Example

"Early in our foray into holistic mind-body-spirit approaches to our problems with sex, we were stuck in a reactive loop. I kept telling Kris 'Nothing is happening' or 'I am not feeling anything' when he would touch my body. From there I would spiral into frustration and despair. At the same time, Kris would notice my body <u>was</u> responding to his touch via shivers and goosebumps, despite what I was telling him. Unbeknownst to us at the time, this mind and body disconnect is a classic symptom of a frozen nervous system.

"After a history of faking climaxes, I had committed to him and to us to be truthful in my experience. It occurred to us that when my mind would wrap itself in work worries or my self-critical 'Nothing is happening' loop, we could apply an adaptation of a mindfulness meditation to call me back into what was true in the present moment by naming what could be seen or felt. For many months, all I was able to say with full honesty was 'I feel my back against the sheets' or 'I feel my butt against the bed.' As embarrassing as that was, I stayed present to that truth. In turn, Kris would lovingly offer, 'I see goosebumps on your thigh. Can you feel them?' and I would bring my attention to my thigh to record in my mind what goosebumps felt like. In moments when I was caught in my loop, I would tell him, 'I am stuck in my head. Help me come back!'

"Then one day something new emerged. I found myself asking him, 'I feel a ghost-like sensation moving down my left inner thigh. Do I have goosebumps there?' He checked and delightedly answered YES!"

Insights Gained Through the Third about Sensation

By learning to sit in the discomfort of an experience, you can access a spectrum of truths about yourself in relationship.

1) First, there is simple recognition: "What is occurring now is outside of my comfort zone." That one recognition is powerful because all of a sudden, you are no longer forcing the other person to conform to your own comfortable box or be subject to emotional turmoil because they don't. You can stand firm in the acknowledgment that "What just happened is neither good nor bad. I don't have to change it. And I don't have to be at the mercy of my 'not liking it' reaction."

2) By acknowledging the landscape of sensations within you and developing a vocabulary for them, you gain access to a moment-by-moment truth. Since it is from this truth that your reactions arise, recognizing the sensation by itself and for itself has the effect of breathing a pause into the space between what is and a chain reaction to address the resulting discomfort. It is in this space that a new outcome can arise.

3) Every time this pause occurs, you are expanding your comfort zone to let a little more of life in.

4) By dropping underneath what you may most often pay attention to, the words, the tone, the action, you see the multitude of layers in which relationship is truly occurring.

This is the rich multi-hued tapestry that relationship becomes through Third Consciousness.

Third Consciousness is Felt

Since life and relationship are experienced through the body as sensation, Third Consciousness is also experienced as sensation. **Gaining a facility with sensations will help you recognize when you are in Third Consciousness, and thus is another doorway**. As you have more and more experiences of relating to others while embodying this consciousness, the felt sense becomes its own barometer, leading to less dependence upon the list of Coherence Signposts. You can cultivate the ability to both feel when you have dropped out, and to navigate back into Third Consciousness through the felt sense in your body memory.

For this reason, it is important to keep paying conscious attention to your body to check what things feel like. At first, this requires slowing things down to create the space to do so, but as you get more skilled, the felt sense will become second nature and will start to guide you. Then the list of Coherence Signposts from the exercise in the previous chapter can serve to help you interpret and calibrate your felt senses: "This is what Third Consciousness feels like" and "This is what incoherence feels like".

Embodied Learning: Sensations Exercise

Set aside 10 minutes for this exercise. Have a copy of the Sensation List from the end of this chapter next to you. If you want a hardcopy, you can download and print it from our website at: http://www.sparkingrelationship.com/rr-one

This practice is called Body Scanning. First refresh your vocabulary of sensations by reading through the Sensation List. Next, start the Body Scan with heart-focused breathing because the heart acts like an orchestra conductor for the body and will help you connect your thinking-mind and your body. You may recognize this first step from the *HeartMath Quick Coherence®️ Technique* introduced in the previous chapter.

1. Focus your attention on your chest, around the area of the heart. Imagine your breath is flowing in and out of your heart, breathing a little slower and deeper than usual. *Suggestion: Inhale 5 seconds, exhale 5 seconds (or whatever rhythm is comfortable.)*

2. Slowly move your attention to your feet to begin the Body Scanning. With a softened attention, what sensations do you notice? If you can, say out loud what sensations you are noticing and where.

3. Now move your attention to your thighs and repeat the process of noticing sensations and saying them out loud.

Continue to work your way up into your butt, abdomen, chest, shoulders, neck and head. Make sure to include your arms and hands.

4. As you become more proficient at Body Scanning, include parts of your body that you rarely notice, such as your right calf or left ear or forearms.

Initially, you may only recognize sensations of temperature or of something pressing against your skin. We have found that people start recognizing more and more sensations with practice and when they have the time and space to do so. As you get familiar with this process, you may find that you no longer need the Sensations List and it will take less and less time for you to notice your sensations – especially the 2-3 peak sensations that are most intense. By repeating this exercise the range of sensations you find comfortable will expand. As you do this, you are opening yourself to the present moment, to more truth, and to Third Consciousness.

Relationship as Practice

Small steps result in big changes over time. Paying attention, being astonished, and telling someone about it are great ways to integrate skills you develop in getting to or remaining in Third Consciousness. This expands the limits of the thinking-mind, and teaches it how to access Third Consciousness. Here are some things to notice:

1. Notice your sensations when you are doing something pleasurable like eating a delicious meal. Name them and

state where they are located in your body. Did you notice sensations throughout your body or mainly in your mouth through taste?

2. See if you can notice your sensations when you are interacting with someone that you know. What is it like to notice your sensations while interacting with someone?

3. If you have been doing the practice of creating pauses during your day to use your Coherence Signposts (from the previous chapter), let's modify that practice. Throughout the day, upon determining whether you are in coherence or not using your signposts, instead of using the *HeartMath Quick Coherence® Technique*, try doing a Body Scan to notice which sensations might be associated with coherence versus incoherence. Note these down on your Coherence Signposts list. By doing this, you will develop the felt sense of when you are in or out of coherence.

Sensations

I feel a xxxx, yyyyy sensation in my (specific location in your body)

Location	Temperature	Texture	Motion	Vibration	Pleasure/pain
Back	Chilly	Abrasive	Accelerating	Buzzing	Achy
Chest	Cold	Buttery	Ascending	Fluttery	Antsy
Ear	Glowing	Caramel	Bursting	Intermittent	Burning
Face	Hot	Crackling	Constricting	Jittery	Crampy
Feet	Icy	Drenched	Contracting	Oscillating	Electric
Finger	Melting	Dull	Dragging	Pulsating	Growly
Hand	Warm	Fuzzy	Dripping	Quivering	Intense
Heart		Gritty	Effervescent	Shaky	Irritating
Hip	**Taste/Flavor**	Knotted	Falling	Shivery	Itchy
Neck	Acidic	Meaty	Fizzy	Staccato	Numb
Toe	Bitter	Melty	Friction	Throbbing	Prickly
	Buttery	Metallic	Grinding	Trembling	Queasy
Shape	Caramel	Misty	Gushing	Vibrating	Scratchy
Diffused	Creamy	Moist	Jolting	Zinging	Soothing
Boundless	Crisp	Mushy	Jumpy		Stinging
Circle	Dry	Nubbly	Languid	**Pressure**	Tender
Cocooned	Honeyed	Plush	Massaging	Buoyant	Tickly
Column	Quenched	Rough	Opening	Clamping	Tingling
Deep	Syrup	Sandpapery	Rising	Dense	
Elevated	Tangy	Sharp	Rotating	Empty	
Elongated		Silky	Shooting	Engorged	
Flat	**Color**	Smooth	Spiraling	Explosive	
Hollow	Blue	Soft	Steady	Full	
Line	Bright	Sparkly	Streaming	Heavy	
Precise	Clear	Steel	Swirling	Implosive	
Shallow	Dark	Velvety	Whooshing	Light	
Spherical	Glowing	Watery	Wobbly	Limp	
Spikey	Luminescent	Wet	Zapping	Loose	
Tubular	Obscure			Open	
Undulating	Red			Pinching	
Zigzag				Tight	

5. THE ENERGETICS OF THE SPACE BETWEEN

Unexpectedly, our Council practice effortlessly spilled over into our daily lives: the deep listening, dropping into the truth of a sensation and feeling the dissonance of an incoherent reaction all melded into a state of being with which we interacted with each other and people we encountered. We began to gain proficiency with Third Consciousness and to recognize its guidance in our daily lives, even in our choices for personal growth work we chose to pursue. The Third was guiding us to teachers and practices that would reveal other unrecognized barriers that our thinking-minds had in place.

We had the privilege to be in a small group spending the morning learning from Jack Canfield, the author of the "Chicken Soup of the Soul" series. Jack asked a volunteer to stand next to him and raise her arm to shoulder height. He asked us to think supportive loving thoughts about the volunteer. We could see that her arm remained strong as Jack applied gentle pressure.

Then, Jack asked us to make up vile, hurtful, angry thoughts about the volunteer and silently hurl them at her. This time her arm dropped! Jack encouraged her repeatedly to lift her arm but in the presence of our silent barrage, she couldn't! When he asked us to stop, her arm began to lift slowly but it was obvious that she was using a lot of effort for a small amount of movement. Jack asked us to beam love on her, and she could resume moving her arm as she had at the beginning.

Jack explained that everything has an impact on the body's electrical field. If something maintains or enhances your body, then your muscles will remain strong. If it adversely impacts your body, your muscles will temporarily weaken. By him gently pressing on the volunteer's arm, all of us could assess the impact.

That's when we pierced an unseen barrier that had been limiting us. The barrier was the erroneous belief that we only impact each other by what is said and done. As we turned to look at each other, we heard the Third say, "Yes! It is true! You <u>are</u> more connected than you realize!"

Up until that moment, we were operating under the understanding that "My reaction is <u>completely</u> my own". Now we saw a nuanced "Yes, and" that the Third affirmed. <u>Yes</u>, your reaction <u>does</u> arise from within you based on your personal comfort zone of sensations. <u>And</u>, we all impact each other with more than just our words, tone, and actions: we impact each other with the quality of our thoughts and emotions.

****

The Space Between

Another intimate realm of the Third is the Space Between you and another person, beyond what your dominant senses of sight and hearing tell you.

Scientists have found that heartbeats create an energetic field around each of us that can be measured many feet past the outside of our bodies. You read in an earlier chapter that your thoughts and emotions are coded in the rhythm of your heartbeats. Putting these two concepts together, it must be recognized and acknowledged that we all transmit our thoughts and emotions into the Space Between us, even when we are not consciously doing or saying anything. Take that in for a moment. You unknowingly transmit your thoughts and feelings through an invisible energetic field which others receive.

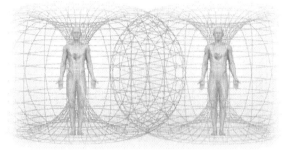

These "transmissions" create a resonance in the energetic field of others. It is like when a tuning fork vibrates the air around it when it is struck, which in-turn then vibrates a nearby tuning fork. Each of us subconsciously senses this resonance through sensations in our body. While this may sound like a superpower that an alien from a science fiction movie might have, the truth is that our bodies are actually that magical.

Each of us has our own thoughts and feelings in reaction to what we sense in the Space Between us. These thoughts and feelings are then transmitted back by our heartbeats, and a cycle of energetic communication is created. Hence, there is a constant and complex conversation that goes on between you and those around you, even when you are not consciously doing or saying anything. This conversation is below the level of your typical consciousness. What has become apparent to us as we have been exploring Third Consciousness is that this communication can happen when people are separated by great distances and multiple time zones – so Third Consciousness is beyond space and time. We all are truly more connected than we realize!

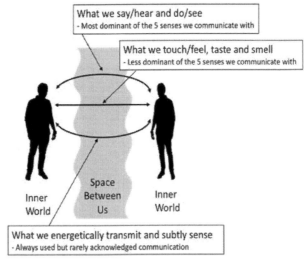

If you are skeptical, we understand. This took a while for us to accept as well. Have you ever walked into a room after a heated argument and could sense the "tension" in the room? Or have you had an experience where someone popped up in your thoughts and seconds later, you got a phone call from them? Or you had the same idea/thought that a close friend had at almost exactly the same time. Until we experienced the Jack Canfield demonstration, it had been easy for us to dismiss these examples as "coincidence". We entered another doorway into a deeper level of Third Consciousness by realizing that these are actually examples of sensing the Space Between you and another person. Hence, the Third shows each of us a deeper level of connection, more so than our dominant senses that tell us we are not connected when we aren't doing or saying something.

> **The Third Perspective:** *You are more connected with others than you realize. Pay attention to what is arising in the space between you.*

Kris' Personal Example

"Years ago, I came home from work frustrated and angry. I had just gotten off a work call with a customer and the call had not gone well. After pulling the car into the garage, I entered through the kitchen. As soon as I entered, Meenal sensed my anger, even though she was working in our home office at the other end of the house and I hadn't said anything. When I made it over to our home office, an argument ensued about something or another. It was only when Meenal paused and asked me whether I had come home angry, that the truth was revealed.

She told me that when she heard the door to the house slam shut, she assumed my anger was directed at her. She shared, 'I had lost track of time and hadn't started preparing dinner.' So, she went on the offensive. When she realized my anger had nothing to do with her, she shifted out of her 'the best defense is a good offense' strategy. By Meenal shifting out of anger, mine shifted very quickly as well. We were both reacting to what was in the space between us, even though it had nothing to do with each other."

Has something similar happened to you, where another person's anger or frustration set you off for no apparent reason?

All It Takes is One Person to Change

Without consciousness, you can fall victim to the effects of this constant and complex energetic conversation. Over time, this energetic conversation can lead to frustrating repeating patterns of behavior in relationship. What can these look like? Have you noticed how, over time, many relationships become infected with criticism and complaints or predictability and boredom? He criticizes, she rolls her eyes. She complains, he deflects or justifies. After hearing 'no' often enough, she thinks she knows his answer even before she asks, so she stops asking. While these are more evident in romantic partnerships, this applies to frustrating repeating patterns in any relationship. Unfortunately, this is the dominant paradigm of relating.

The good news is that merely recognizing the depth of our collective interconnectedness helps to shine light on these stuck patterns. Doing so can take you out the victim role in the pattern and allow you to illuminate the truth and respond differently.

Another powerful way to interrupt a frustrating pattern is by taking responsibility for the quality of thoughts and emotions that you put into the Space Between you and another person. If you were to throw silent daggers of judgment and complaints into the Space Between you and a colleague, it could be just as harmful as if you were doing it out loud. Remember what we described with Jack Canfield and the volunteer?

A starting point in taking responsibility is to ask yourself in any situation, "What could be my part in this?" or "What could I have done differently?" Even if it seems like it is completely someone else's doing, asking either of these questions opens you to the reality of interconnectedness and what you are putting into the Space Between.

> *We are slowed down sound and light waves, a walking bundle of frequencies tuned into the cosmos. We are souls dressed up in sacred biochemical garments and our bodies are the instruments through which our souls play their music.* ~ Albert Einstein

Moving from Independence to Inter-dependence

A lot of personal growth work and work in relationships focuses on supporting people in moving away from co-dependent behaviors and to recognize their independence. While this is empowering and does indeed help break up old stuck patterns that do not serve either person or the relationship, we don't live in a state of independence. We are interconnected and therefore inter-dependent.

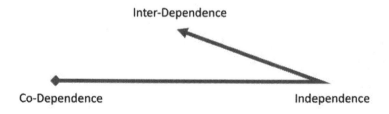

The truth is that both you and the other person always have some part in each interaction, some of it seen and heard through words and body language, and some of it unseen and experienced energetically through the Space Between.

Recognizing this allows all of us to approach relating to others with both responsibility and compassion. It is not about blaming someone else because they are transmitting. Rather, it is about starting to pay attention to what you may be putting into the Space Between in your relationships.

When you accept that you are more interconnected with others than you realize and begin to start acting as if this truth is true, you open a door into a magical world that contains so much more of what relationship has to offer. The energetic connection becomes clear and you start putting attention on creating coherence between you. We discovered that when two or more people are coherent, their creative ability in terms of manifesting a shared vision is substantially enhanced. This is a path into the mystical and the true potential of relationship. While this topic is a passion of ours to explore and teach, we want to prepare you to experience this as you start embracing Third Consciousness, so we leave this topic for a subsequent book.

Relationship as Practice

Remember, small steps result in big changes over time. Paying attention, being astonished, and telling someone about it are great ways to integrate skills you develop in getting to and remaining in Third Consciousness. Here are some things to do and notice:

1. If something challenging arises in a relationship (it may be unexpected or it may be a familiar pattern), rather than reacting, pause for a moment and check in with your sensations. If you have been doing the practice from the last

chapter, this should be a quick process. What are the top three sensations you are feeling right now and where do you feel them?

2. Now ask yourself, "What could be my part in this challenging situation?" or "What could I have done differently?"

3. What shifted for you when you paused to notice your sensations? Did anything else happen when you asked yourself what your part in a challenging relationship situation might have been?

6. What Does it Mean?

When we first began teaching our workshops, we operated under the misperception that Third Consciousness applied only to couples. As much as the marketing was geared towards couples, we were surprised to discover that nearly half of the students who attended were single and wanting to be in relationship. The Third was guiding us to expand our perception of who wanted these teachings.

Many of them shared stories of decades-long rifts with siblings or exiling themselves as the "black-sheep" of the family. Underneath the specifics of the stories, we realized there was a common theme: an experience of betrayal by a family member that they could not navigate past and a sincere desire for a different outcome. Not having experienced exile in our families, all we could do was ask the participants to trust what we had planned for the workshop. When they did, magical insights and dramatic openings appeared for them!

Clearly, they were benefiting from something we were teaching. We wanted to know what that was, so we turned to our Third for answers.

* *

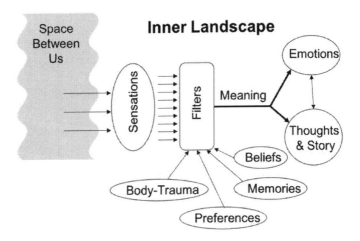

A Common Barrier

We are all bombarded by sensory input. Incoming sensations from the Space Between must be filtered, otherwise they would overwhelm the thinking-mind and effectively incapacitate any of us. This filter discards vast amounts of information based on its criteria of relevance. In the movie, "*What the Bleep Do We Know?*", Dr. Joe Dispenza narrates about how we all receive approximately 400 billion bits of information each second, but this is reduced to about 2,000 bits so our thinking-minds can process it. This means that for every single piece of information that makes it through, almost 200,000 are filtered out.

Another important aspect that occurs as part of this filtering process is that you assign a meaning to everything – we are all meaning making machines. The meaning is used to determine relevance and results in thoughts and stories that validate that meaning.

Your filter is built upon your beliefs, memories, comfort zones, body-held-trauma (stuck energy pattern in the body), and meanings you validated in the past. The nature of your filter and the things that feed into it comprise your inner landscape, which is rarely seen but significantly impacts your experience.

A Practice to Soften the Filter

Believing the meaning and story you assign to an experience can have a profound impact on your emotions. When first starting out on the path to Third Consciousness, it can be difficult to recognize this. Often it seems like the other person or an experience is the direct cause of feeling a certain way. As protection from feeling strong emotions that don't feel good, you may blame people in your life or distance yourself from them. Wouldn't it be wonderful if there was a simple and easy way to soften the grip of those emotions and even recognize their true cause?

Fortunately, it actually is that easy. When strong emotions like frustration, anger, anxiety, or fear come up, instead of leaping into action, you can bring mindfulness into the equation by asking yourself, "What is the meaning (or story) I am believing right now?" This simple question can help you recognize that so many of the emotions you feel are closely tied to the meaning you have assigned to an experience and the story you created around that meaning. In the process of asking that question, you slow things down and give yourself the chance to feel the sensations of your emotions. **The question is a doorway into Third Consciousness because you are asking to see things from the Third's vantage point.** Over time, making a practice of asking yourself this question can help you soften, pause, and discern what actually happened from the story you created.

Our Need to Belong

We are all built on a desire to survive – it is in our nature. Not that long ago, survival meant that we needed to belong to a group. Human beings evolved to become social creatures to survive in a world where we were potential prey and to hunt larger, stronger and faster animals by working in groups. Since the need for belonging has been built into each of us, we still rely on it to feel safe – especially emotionally. One way human beings learned to belong was to seek out others like them. The residual of this is that we all tend to gravitate to people that are like us and assume that the people we associate with think and feel exactly as we do.

A Betrayal

A further stumbling block in relating occurs when you believe the meaning or story you create as the only perspective. This naturally leads to assuming that everyone in your tribe of friends and family must believe it as well. Based on the innate need for belonging, a natural conclusion is that if someone agrees with your meaning / story, then they are "for you" (they belong with you) and therefore, "love you". When the opposite occurs and they disagree, you might perceive a betrayal has occurred because this person you love is now "against you". Some people find themselves exiling family members (or themselves from family) because their beliefs and feelings about a situation are different than their own.

From the Third's vantage point, what actually occurred is a betrayal of the assumption "If you love me, you will believe, think, and act the way I do." The reality is that your filter will necessarily be different than someone else's because you are different people. Each of your filters are based on a lifetime of experiences and beliefs and meanings that you have assigned. All you can truly know is that you cannot rely on the meaning and story that you assigned as the truth or the <u>right</u> perspective.

Just realizing the existence of the filter helps soften the "betrayal" of family and friends that came from expectations that their inner landscape was the same as yours. Knowing about filters can lead to more compassion and curiosity when someone reacts differently than you do. **Compassion and curiosity are signposts of Third Consciousness.**

Meenal's Personal Example

"When we got the first proofs of this book, I wanted to share my excitement with family here in the US and in India. I posted a photo of the book in my extended family's WhatsApp thread. Within minutes, I started receiving excited congratulations from cousins, aunts, nieces and nephews. And yet, what struck me was that Amma [my mother], who actively engages in all topics ranging from Who's Who in family photos to current movies to puzzles to wishing people on their birthdays, did not say anything. At first, I felt confused, but after a few days I began to feel hurt with a twinge of betrayal creeping in.

"I emptied out numerous times, but the hurt persisted. When I boiled it all down, my mind couldn't come up with a meaning other than she didn't care, that could explain her silence on this one topic. I realized that I could let my mind keep spinning by staying silent or I could say something to her without any blame, simply sharing that I felt hurt. When I did, she immediately responded, 'I tried to text you directly. Not on the family thread. Maybe I didn't. I am sorry!

"Because I refused to believe the meaning my mind was stuck with, I could receive her sincere words and feel the loving balm of them melt away my hurt."

> **The Third Perspective:** *It is through the diversity of others' perspectives that you can find the magic in life and can get to know Third Consciousness better.*

Relationship as Practice

Remember, small steps result in big changes over time. Paying attention, being astonished, and telling someone about it are great ways to integrate skills you develop in getting to or remaining in Third Consciousness. This expands the limits of the thinking-mind, and teaches it how to access Third Consciousness. Here are some things to do and notice:

1. When you notice yourself having a strong reaction, briefly pause and ask yourself "What meaning have I applied to

this?" If emotions like frustration, anger or fear come up, ask yourself a simple question, "What is the story I am telling myself right now?" Notice how your story or the meaning may be impacting the emotions you are feeling. Does the grip of the story or emotion soften when you realize this connection?

2. If there is someone that you think betrayed you, consider what they did with curiosity about their inner landscape that led them to the action they took. If you feel courageous, ask them to help you understand their perspective.

7. THE DOORWAY OF FORGIVENESS

One December, we decided to attend a Winter Cleanse Retreat offered over the New Year's holiday. Due to our respective health challenges, we had participated in numerous food-related cleanses over the years, but we had never done one in community. We were drawn to the idea of starting the new year feeling clean, crisp, and bright, surrounded by redwood trees. Unbeknownst to us, this would be a cleanse unlike any we had experienced before!

The morning after we arrived, we discovered that our cleanse had nothing to do with food. Instead, we were going to take 2 days to review all of our relationships to create a complete inventory of disconnecting thoughts and behaviors, and how it had served our egos to perpetuate them. We would feel cleansed by this process.

There were many times when we were confronted by this endeavor, but we agreed to stick it out. After all, we were deep in Third Consciousness, so how many of these could we still have? Quite a few - two days' worth, in fact.

The more we excavated, revealed, acknowledged, and mourned; the lighter, happier, and clearer we felt. It was like we had scrubbed through a thick build-up that we didn't realize was there, only to discover a deep, crisp, fresh, effervescent well-spring of love that bubbled out of us and spilled over onto everything and everyone around us. The only thing that had changed was us.

During the long car ride home, we were trying to put into words what we had experienced. We realized that the Third can see both the build-up and what's underneath, so how could we tap into this wisdom. It was then that we intuitively got our surprising answer.

****

Residue – an Invisible Barrier

Have you ever had judgmental thoughts about something a friend or family member did and although you did your best to express yourself in a loving way, it led to an argument? You may have been affected by residue.

Residue is an invisible sludge within you that colors how you interpret your sensations from the Space Between and also colors your intended responses (thoughts, emotions and actions). Residue builds up from all of the times that you have thought and/or behaved as if you are not interconnected. It can occur from the falsity of independence in your not accepting your impact on others. It also results from codependent behaviors, like when Kris jumped in to fix Meenal's work-related challenge without Meenal asking (as we wrote about in Chapter 4). It also occurs from all the times you believed the meaning and story you created from your filter.

A simple way to think about this is that residue is your attachment to protection-based thoughts and behaviors and every action you took in the past strengthened this attachment. Therefore, residue is a barrier within you that keeps you from Third Consciousness. During that Winter Cleanse Retreat, we were unknowingly excavating and clearing residue.

The easiest way to recognize that you have residue is by noticing resentment. For us, a resentment is "a re-sending of a thought or emotion". It could be the fuming that occurs long after an interaction. It could be the repeated "I wish I had said xxxx!". It could be bringing up something that happened a few weeks ago in today's argument. Or it could be as subtle as mild resignation wrapped around "It doesn't matter what I do. They won't change." Remember the Third IS the infinite field of possibilities in every relationship. As long as you have resentments, you are not fully seated in Third Consciousness.

> *Your task is not to seek for love, but merely to seek and find all the barriers within yourself that you have built against it.* ~ Rumi

The True Meaning of Forgiveness

An article in *Greater Good Magazine,* a publication of the Greater Good Science Center at the University of California Berkeley, defines forgiveness as "a conscious, deliberate decision to release feelings of resentment ... toward a person or group who has harmed you, regardless of whether they actually deserve your forgiveness." The article says that forgiveness is not denying the seriousness of an offense against you. "Forgiveness does not mean forgetting, nor does it mean condoning or excusing offenses. Though forgiveness can help repair a damaged relationship, it doesn't obligate you to reconcile with the person who harmed you."

So, what damaged relationship do you think is being repaired? This isn't damage in your relationship with the other person, though that is what it often seems like. It is actually a tear between you and the Third. From the Third Perspective, **clearing residue and its resulting resentment eliminates the one remaining barrier between you and full alignment with Third Consciousness.** It is a pure form of forgiveness, that originates from a natural impulse to come back fully into Love. Thus, **true forgiveness is a doorway to Third Consciousness.**

> **The Third Perspective:** *Forgive yourself, as you are already forgiven by me. Everyone engages in those old behaviors. You didn't know there was another way. Forgive and experience who I know you to be.*

A Simple Forgiveness Practice

You might be thinking to yourself, "These are great points, but I need to know how to do it, because otherwise it becomes another thing I **should** do". We have a very practical solution - a Hawaiian practice of reconciliation and forgiveness called Ho'oponopono, which we modified with tools and concepts you have learned in this book.

The Hawaiian word Ho'oponopono translates into English simply as *adjustment* while its antonym is *careless*. Historically, it was a practice of extended family members meeting to "make right" broken family relations. Some families met daily to prevent relationship problems from erupting. Others met when a person became ill, believing that illness was caused by the stress (from anger or guilt) and lack of forgiveness. Does any of this sound similar to what you have read in this book?

Embodied Learning: Modified Ho'oponopono Practice

Set aside 10 minutes for this exercise. Recall a protection-based behavior that you participated in over the last couple of days. Create a simple 2-5 word description (e.g. judging my friend, believing the meaning I created, insisting I was right, etc).

1) You will start this exercise with the *HeartMath Quick Coherence® Technique* introduced in Chapter 3. Do this for about 5 minutes.

   Step 1: Focus your attention in the area of the heart. Imagine your breath is flowing in and out of your heart or chest area, breathing a little slower and deeper than usual. *Suggestion: Inhale 5 seconds, exhale 5 seconds (or whatever rhythm is comfortable.)*

   Step 2: Make a sincere attempt to experience a regenerative feeling such as appreciation or care for someone or something in your life. *Suggestion: Try to re-experience the feeling you have for someone you love, a pet, a special place, an accomplishment, etc. or focus on a feeling of calm or ease.*

2) Imagine you are speaking to the Third and repeat the following sequence 10 times, allowing yourself to fully feel and express the meaning of the words:
   a) I am sorry for separating from you by [say the simple description of your protection-based behavior]
   b) Please forgive me, I want to reconnect with you
   c) Thank you, I open my heart with gratitude
   d) I love you

3) Notice your sensations after this exercise.

Relationship as Practice

Small steps result in big changes over time. Paying attention, being astonished, and telling someone about it are great ways to integrate skills you develop in getting to or remaining in Third Consciousness. This expands the limits of the thinking-mind, and teaches it how to access Third Consciousness.

1. If you have been doing the practice of creating pauses during your day to gauge your coherence (from Chapters 3 or 4), let's modify that practice. As you move through your day, if you notice that you are incoherent, keep in mind which behavior from your *Coherence Signposts* sheet most helped you recognize your incoherent state.

2. Do the Modified Ho'oponopono Practice described in this chapter using that incoherent behavior.

3. Notice what sensations you are experiencing. If you have been doing the practice from Chapter 4, are the sensations you felt during that practice when you were in coherence and Third Consciousness similar to those you feel now?

8. ACCEPTANCE AND VULNERABILITY

Through our living breathing practice, we had become fascinated students of relationship. Whenever we encountered something that felt "slightly off" or that resulted in a "huh?" reaction from either of us, we realized there was something new for us to learn. In stepping back and asking to see what we couldn't see, the Third would show us, oftentimes instantaneously.

After a residue revealing exercise during a coaching session, the client profusely thanked Meenal for seeing her and hearing her. Meenal's first reaction was, "Of course!" followed by a "Huh?" moment. The client was in a long-term loving relationship, so why hadn't she felt that from her partner?

The client could reveal to Meenal the residue of annoyance, helplessness, anger, and uncertainty in a way she believed she couldn't with her partner. She feared that her partner's worries would escalate. So the client was holding herself tightly around her partner, pretending that nothing was wrong, and unconsciously using irritation to push her partner away, who in turn would get angry. Hence, the pattern of escalating criticism in an otherwise very loving relationship.

In a flash, Meenal saw what was going on. It was familiar from her own experience with Kris and his medication, except now she saw a nuance that she hadn't seen before. It was the "pretending that nothing was wrong / I don't need you / I am handling this" that was the source of the crazy-making!

****

Is this behavior familiar? Perhaps you think it is not worth revealing what you are truly thinking and feeling because they won't understand. Or perhaps you think that if you revealed your thoughts and emotions, the other person will judge you and may even leave the relationship. The deepest fear that all of us have in relationship is revealing the tenderest part of ourselves and then somehow being rejected.

Do you recall from the chapter entitled "The Energetics of the Space Between" that each of us transmits our thoughts and feelings through our heart beat rhythms? With stronger emotions, these are easily sensed by those around us through the Space Between. The other person may sense when you are angry, sad or brimming with happiness. In meaningful longer-term relationships, what can be sensed can be very subtle. They may not even be able to put words to it, but they likely sense it at some level. It always amazes us that despite knowing this, any of us can still hide our thoughts and emotions by denying them – even when directly asked.

We use the term stonewalling, when it seems that someone erects a barrier to hide what they are thinking or feeling. In the therapy world, stonewalling is defined as 'to delay or block (a request, process, or person) by refusing to answer questions or by giving evasive replies'. It may sound like, "What are you talking about?" or "It's not me, maybe it's you" or "I'm fine" when asked about what's going on. More often than not, in our personal experience, the stonewalling only seems to numb the person that is erecting the barrier, so in effect, they are only hiding from themselves. The crazy-making occurs because the person shut-out on the other side of the wall can actually sense that something is up, but is met with an icy or fiery 'You're wrong' however gently the inquiry is made. There is a very real dissonance that resonates in the Space Between, that is difficult to articulate without cooperation from the person shut within the wall.

Kris's Personal Example

"Shortly before this past New Year's eve, Meenal and I started an envisioning process to bring intention and ceremony into what we are creating in the coming year and new decade. In one of our explorations to set the stage, Meenal started talking about each of us deeply and honestly excavating what is holding us back in bringing these teachings to a broader audience. She pointed out that although we have been coaching people and teaching workshops, we have been quite selective about who we coach and where we teach. Using the reasoning of fit and discernment, were we actually holding ourselves back due to a deeper fear?

"A few days later, while doing my daily HeartMath Coherence practice, I started feeling increasingly agitated. At first, it started as a rumbling in my torso and a jittery feeling in my chest, but then I started having thoughts about how it was Meenal's fears that were holding us back and that she had not been as active as I had on writing this very book and she had been more cautious than I at accepting teaching engagements. The more I focused on my chest and imagined my breath flowing in and out of my heart, the more agitated I seemed to get. I was tapping into something deep within me that I hadn't allowed myself to feel.

"Just then, Meenal walked into the room. She could sense how agitated I was and asked what was wrong. My first reaction was to say 'Nothing, I was just in a deep place in my practice.' Although what I told her was true, I wasn't revealing what was really going on, though it was clear that she sensed something in the Space Between. I started judging the irrationality of my blaming thoughts and in that moment, I truly believed that if I revealed these distasteful thoughts, frustration, and agitation, it would start a fight. I knew she was heading out to a class and I didn't want to pull the pin on the metaphorical grenade I was holding and hand it to her as she was walking out the door.

"As she was putting her shoes on, I realized that the way I had left it with her felt disingenuous, reminiscent of years ago when I would regularly stonewall Meenal. My denying my blaming thoughts was a lie borne from a fear of starting a fight. I also realized that the only way I could release these thoughts was to accept them for what they were by acknowledging them. Luckily, I woke up to the story I was telling myself and chose not to believe it. I quickly went to the front door and told her that although I had been in a deep state in my meditation, I was tapping into frustration and agitation and that I wanted to acknowledge my 'crazy' blaming thoughts. I prefaced these by saying that I own them as thoughts and not as truth, and that my intention wasn't to blame, just to reveal myself. Finally, I outed the story I had created that it was her fears that were slowing us down. I took off my metaphorical armor and became vulnerable.

"Her response was to say 'I hear you and you are right, I own that my fears may have been holding me (and therefore us) back.' I immediately felt my frustration melt and felt a deep sadness emerge around what Meenal must be going through if she was holding us back. The sadness quickly transitioned to an open feeling of being fully accepted for all the parts of me – even my darker blaming thoughts that moments earlier I was having trouble accepting. After Meenal left, I was able to release any remaining charge through a partnered residue revealing practice with a close friend. I was able to see a deeper truth about what my underlying fears were and how they were slowing us down as well."

> **The Third Perspective:** *Your inner-most thoughts and feelings are in the Space Between. Accepting them and courageously revealing them is the only path to being fully accepted and loved by others.*

You may be sensing this already. From the Third's vantage point, all of the behavior that we engage in either stem from a pure expression or love or are distorted because they are rooted in protection. The Third doesn't judge this because learning to distinguish that for ourselves is the very reason relationship exists. If the Third sees and accepts all of them through a lens of compassion and understanding, then there is an inevitability that emerges via Third Consciousness: that it is only a matter of time before you align your behaviors with the truth of interconnectedness and drop those that stem from old paradigms of relating. In this case, if the other person can sense that something is up for me, then what purpose does it serve me to pretend that everything is okay? Acceptance and vulnerability are what remain when I make the choice to lay down my protection.

Each of our inner landscapes is the very real cascade that begins with sensations and leaps to thoughts, emotions and actions, through a complex filter and a self-created meaning. True vulnerability begins by courageously accepting and revealing this inner landscape, first to ourselves and then to others.

We are not advocating that you bring this level of vulnerability to everyone because some peoples' protective mechanisms might harm you when you are open. The first step is a willingness to silently acknowledge "I am feeling frustrated right now. I have blaming thoughts that are popping up and I don't want to believe them. I just want to accept that they are arising, in order to release the grip they have on me." This begins to melt the shame associated with the parts of ourselves we keep hidden.

If something like this is coming up in a relationship where there is a mutual desire to go deeper – say with a romantic partner, a family member, or a close friend, this is the opening for you to add, "Something is churning for me. I would like to share it with you. All I need for you to do is listen to me. There is nothing that you need to fix for me." This begins to exercise the muscle of courage and vulnerability. We have found that taking this on as a practice in one relationship develops a sense of safety that expands to all relationships.

The Third constantly invites each of us to see more of ourselves and to accept ourselves in a way that leads to the safety needed to reveal what's really going on inside. When you deny what you are thinking or feeling because you think it is inappropriate, or when you believe that you won't be accepted for what you are feeling or thinking, you create an environment for shame to fester. Shame is like a sticky, slimy tar and has the ability to hide deeper parts of you from yourself. By revealing the feelings as "just are" without further explanation or story and revealing the thoughts and story you create without believing them, you normalize them and create safety in your relationships, where shame cannot thrive. This leads to more intimacy and a deeper connection with Third Consciousness.

> *We cultivate love when we allow our most vulnerable and powerful selves to be deeply seen and known, and when we honor the spiritual connection that grows from that offering with trust, respect, kindness and affection.* ~ Brené Brown

Relationship as Practice

Remember, small steps can result in big changes over time, and paying attention, being astonished, and telling someone about it are great ways to integrate skills you develop in getting to or remaining in Third Consciousness. Here are some things to do and notice:

1. Notice in your daily routine of relating with others, whether you have judgmental thoughts or uncomfortable feelings that you are not willing to reveal. Acknowledge for yourself what

you are feeling and the associated thoughts. Notice what sensations you felt that were associated with those feelings. You might even ask yourself what meaning you created that might be leading to all of this. You may want to quickly jot the sensations, thoughts and feelings down for later exploration.

2. When you have some privacy to be able to say things to yourself out loud, pull out the notes you made and say "I was feeling _____. I had judgmental thoughts that _____ and _____ that were popping up because the story I created was _____ and I don't want to believe it. I just want to accept that this was arising." As you get more skilled at this, you can try saying it silently to yourself in the moment, when you notice them. Doing it in the moment is especially powerful, as it quickly shines a light on the dark places that shame likes to lurk. Notice what sensations you feel when you do this part of the exercise.

9. ATTENTION: SLOW DOWN

Increasingly, we each had been receiving feedback from those around us that they experienced something palpably different when they are with us. This feedback showed up in various guises, like "I normally wouldn't say this, but ..." or "I know I can tell you this." We even found ourselves sitting at outdoor cafes with friends comfortably talking about traditionally taboo topics. How far we had come from where we had started! We realized that people felt safe with us because we would naturally embody Third Consciousness, where most everything can be seen and held with love.

Despite a certain level of skillfulness, the writing of this book was new territory for us, fraught with gullies that we fell into before finding our way out. It took us 9 months to navigate them, with Kris wanting to push ahead and Meenal applying the brakes. With the publication deadline looming, tension would arise every time we needed to discuss the book. It felt like we were walking on egg-shells. And yet there was a very real issue in one of the chapters that needed to be resolved. Every time Meenal would request content changes, Kris understandably reacted as if she were getting in the way of finishing this by questioning what he had written.

She would ask to sit in Council. We would come to what felt like an agreement and within an hour, he was consumed with a burst of inspired writing. And yet the rewrite still didn't feel on point to her. So the cycle would repeat. We hadn't experienced this magnitude of tense disagreement in many years. There was something here for us to learn, but we kept sliding past it. Logic would suggest that what we should have done in this time compressed pressure cooker was to speed up and focus more on writing. We did exactly the opposite – we slowed WAY down and listened even more deeply. We tapped into how the Third was guiding us to create a flow in the book that was missing, yet needed. What emerged was a clarity for each chapter and how various chapters were tied together. Slowing down helped us listen not just to what edits each of us was suggesting, but what each of us was sensing from the Third. We not only got on the same page with each other, but we got on the same page with the Third.

* *

Have you ever wanted to have a "heart-to-heart" talk with someone, but after starting the conversation, you feel like they are distracted? Or perhaps because the other person is always so busy, you blurted out something deeply meaningful because you didn't know when would be a good time? Pressing forward and sharing what you want to say may have felt unsatisfying or perhaps even hurtful – like you weren't getting the attention you needed.

How would you have felt if that person had said to you, "I want to have this conversation, but I need to finish this right now. Can we create sacred space this afternoon because I want to give you my undivided attention?" In receiving that as an answer, do your shoulders soften or a relaxation spread through your body in knowing that the chances of you being heard have sky-rocketed?

> **The Third Perspective:** *Attention is a nutrient that feeds your relationships, and thus Me. Offering others high quality attention will bring you closer to Me.*

We have already explored the impact of judgmental thoughts in the Space Between, the impact of residue, and the power of forgiveness. So, what is left after you have reconnected with the Third through the Ho'oponopono practice? Pure, loving, curious attention. Meenal experiences this quality of attention as warmer and more palpable than the detached witnessing attention that is accessed via some forms of meditation. This is not a highly-focused attention like someone may apply when trying to solve a problem. It is more like noticing the big picture while also noticing subtle details. **This warm curious attention is a signpost of Third Consciousness.** It is characterized by an intuitively-motivated "What's happening now?" and a desire to discover more; a complete absence of an impulse to fix or change. This quality of attention is grounded in a pure pleasure of facilitating a de-armoring to reveal what's underneath, almost like watching a present being unwrapped. It is from this state that both the intimate and the infinite can be accessed. If you have been practicing the various embodied learning exercises, chances are you have become familiar with this quality of attention.

Dr. Jill Bolte Taylor, a neuroscientist who gave the famous TED talk titled *"My Stroke of Insight"* about when she was hospitalized and in a comatose state, spoke about how she could viscerally sense the difference between staff who thought, "She's in a coma so she is a vegetable" and those who thought, "She's in a coma but she is still a living breathing human being." She actually did not feel physically safe with the former group because the quality of their attention was palpably different - distracted, dismissive, brusque, abrupt. This was the very opposite of warm, curious, and caring attention, which is what she felt from the second group.

If this quality of attention truly is that vital and can be felt, how often do any of us actually offer that in our relationships? While it is sometimes given to a child, a pet, or a sick person while caring for them; in the rush of modern life with more and more distractions and pressure, your ability to bring it into your relationships is compromised. So, what can you do?

Slow Things Down

Your access to attention increases when you slow things down and minimize distractions. Nearly ten years ago, we came across a simple ritual of visually and viscerally creating a "Sacred Space" where we would intentionally slow things down and implicitly and explicitly agree to take out the distractions, interruptions, and stresses of everyday life. This powerful 5-minute practice freed up our attention so it could be offered to facilitate deep listening and sharing. It has become an oasis that travels with us, wherever in the world we are, even if we are geographically apart. It is a way that we both demonstrate (via the invitation to create Sacred Space) and feel (via the resulting attentive listening) the love that we have for each other. On a non-verbal viscerally-felt level, we are telling each other, "You matter to me. I am willing to put everything aside to be fully here with you." We give each other this vital nutrient so that we can return to our other relationships filled more fully with the compassion and love we want to offer others. We have also found that as we practiced offering curious attention in this Sacred Space, we cultivated and expanded our capacity for attention, to be able to offer it in more and more situations, despite the distractions and rush of modern life.

In the past year, we have not only taught this practice in all of our workshops, but also introduced this practice to friends and family around the world. Most people report feeling calmer, more present, centered, and grounded. One friend in particular has been using it actively to heal dysfunctional patterns in her family dynamics. After weeks of using a partnered forgiveness practice which resulted in her seeing and mourning her part in a family dynamic, she invited that person to create Sacred Space with her and to begin courageously revealing the filter-driven story she had been believing about the other person, adding in "I am sharing because I don't want this to continue. You matter to me." And then she listened. Meenal feels so blessed to be one of the people with whom she shares the resulting miracles!

Embodied Learning: Creating Sacred Space Ritual

This exercise of creating sacred space will add 5-10 minutes to a conversation you wish to have with a partner. In this sacred space you can give your partner high quality attention while they share what is most meaningful for them and you can share your more tender parts with a better chance of being heard and understood.

1) Close your eyes and connect with yourself through Heart-Focused Breathing.
   a) Focus your attention on your chest, around the area of the heart. Imagine your breath is flowing in and out of your heart, breathing a little slower and deeper than usual. *Suggestion: Inhale 5 seconds, exhale 5 seconds (or whatever rhythm is comfortable.)*

2) Open your eyes when you feel a deeper connection with yourself. Wait until your partner has opened his/her eyes before proceeding.

3) Connect with your partner via a Heart Salutation.
   a) Look into each other's eyes.

   b) Bring your hands together in prayer position, first with fingertips touching the ground. As you inhale together, raise your hands to your heart level, while maintaining prayer position and eye contact.

   c) As you exhale together, slowly bow your heads towards each other until your foreheads touch while maintaining eye contact. As your foreheads touch, take one more deep breath in and let it out.

   d) On the next inhale, raise yourself back to an upright seated position while maintaining eye contact.

e) On the final exhale, lower your hands maintaining prayer position with the fingertips touching the ground.

4) Connect with The Third by creating a bubble.

a) Raise your arms above your head and use your fingertips to symbolically trace the edges of a bubble that surrounds you, your partner and The Third. Within the bubble, you are now in Sacred Space, consciously separated from the ordinary, the mundane, the routine.

b) "Remove" what could get in your way of being present by taking turns naming a fear, worry or distraction (e.g. "I am removing having to get it right", "I am removing time pressure", "I remove fear that I will be misunderstood", etc.) while using an arm gesture as if you are moving it from the Space Between you to outside the bubble. Continue until you both feel that everything that needs to be named, has been.

c) Bring in the qualities you desire to experience in Sacred Space by taking turns naming these qualities (e.g. "I bring in understanding", "I bring in deep listening", etc.) while using an arm gesture as if you were moving it from outside the bubble into the Space Between you. Continue until you both feel that everything that you desire to include has been included.

When you are complete with giving each other the quality of attention that you want and each of you have said what you need to say, you may close Sacred Space with a Heart Salutation (Step 3 above) and a symbolic popping of the bubble by reaching up above your heads with a finger flick, like you are popping a soap bubble.

When you first start using this ritual, pay particular attention to what you sense in the Space Between before and after the ritual. Does it feel different?

Although initially this ritual may add 10 minutes to your conversation, as you become skilled at doing this, you will find that it goes much more quickly because it can take on a flavor of fun and whimsy. You can also play with setting a timer to allow you to free up even more attention and fully relax into the Sacred Space, while still not losing sight of things on your to-do list. This ritual can also be used with groups.

We are friends with a couple with whom we have a monthly video call. It used to be that the calls were filled with catching up and chatting, a narration of what had transpired between the calls. Over time, Meenal noticed that she wasn't looking forward to the calls in the way she would have expected given the depth of this friendship. On the next call, she asked that we create Sacred Space together. At the end of the call, all of us agreed that the rhythm felt deeper and richer, more in keeping with the connection we have had when we have seen each other in person. We all agreed that we would do this with every call.

We want to bring your attention to the fundamentals in the Sacred Space Ritual. When you "remove" things that could get in the way of your being fully present from the Space Between, these are signs of incoherence that get in the way of your connecting with the Third. Through the process of removing, you are practicing acceptance and vulnerability. Acceptance because you are acknowledging and accepting the existence of barriers you brought into the Space Between, and vulnerability because you are sharing that they are keeping you from Third Consciousness. When you "bring in" qualities you desire more of, these are typically qualities of Third Consciousness. You are therefore creating an intention to connect with the Third.

The Sacred Space Ritual is highly effective at creating an environment that helps people connect with Third Consciousness. However, we realize that there are situations where it might be awkward to introduce this ritual into an interaction - a conversation with a colleague, for example. Relying on the fundamentals of the Sacred Space Ritual, we created another method to create sacred space in almost any situation.

Embodied Learning: Sacred Space Incognito

Take 2 minutes to try this simple exercise when you first get together with a friend, family member, or even a colleague. They don't have to be aware of what you are doing. Remember, all it takes is one person to change, so even your silently using this technique will have an impact.

1) Connect with yourself through Heart-Focused Breathing while keeping your eyes open.
   a) Focus your attention on your chest, around the area of the heart. Imagine your breath is flowing in and out of your heart, breathing a little slower and deeper than usual. *Suggestion: Inhale 5 seconds, exhale 5 seconds (or whatever rhythm is comfortable.)*

2) Connect with The Third via your breath.
   a) Notice any thoughts or feelings that are distracting you
      from being present. "Remove" them by imagining that
      you are breathing them out with each out breath (e.g.
      breathe out frazzled feeling and thoughts about the
      person that cut you off in traffic).

   b) Choose one or two qualities or attitudes that you want to
      "bring in" to your sacred space. Imagine breathing them
      in with each in breath (e.g. breathe in ease and
      attention).

3) If you feel it is appropriate for the circumstance, you can
   acknowledge out loud some feelings and intentions in a
   conversational style. Examples:
   a) "I am feeling frazzled because traffic was heavy and I
      arrived a few minutes late."

   b) "I want to let this go so I can easily give you my full
      attention to fully understand what you want to tell me."

State the Truth of What Is

The reality is that each of us moves in and out of Third
Consciousness, based on how resourced we are. If you are tired,
it will be more difficult to offer quality attention for an extended
period of time, than when you are fresh and awake. If you are
feeling the pressure of "too much going on", you will be less able
to focus on what is being said by the person in front of you. If
you feel a strong emotional reaction like anger or frustration, or

judgmental thoughts occurring in you based on what was just shared, you are on the edge of leaving Third Consciousness. In other words, the quality of your attention will be affected by what's going on within you.

We all feel each other. So, any of us can sense the subtle attention wobble in the other person, even if we don't quite know what's going on. Invariably, rather than granting the other person space to tend to their wobble or to inquire "What's going on with you right now?", we often push ahead because "I don't know when I will get your attention next!" or defensively stiffen by thinking "I must not matter enough to you".

You may wonder how feeling sensation in your body and knowing you have filters is relevant in daily interactions. On one hand, each are ways to bring curious attention into yourself. On another hand, they are tools to help you stay grounded in what is happening within you because that is what you are bringing to the present moment interaction. When you realize you are the one with the attention wobble, the kindest thing to do is to name the truth of what is happening within you, "I am feeling tired. Even though I want to continue this, the tiredness is getting in my way." The way the other person knows they can trust your sincerity is by making sure to follow your statement of "what is" with, "Can we come back in [a specified time] after I have [what you need to do to allow you to be fully present]?"

In this moment, you are effectively communicating a boundary via a "Now is no longer a good time for me". And yet, this surface level "no" is actually a "yes" to a deeper, truer form of relationship - one that is based in the quality of attention that you want to offer, and a commitment to speak up when you are not able to offer it. **Sensing what is arising in the present moment is another doorway to Third Consciousness.** The act of naming it, which brings it to everyone's consciousness, and making choices/requests based on that truth, results in a different outcome. The more proficient you become at noticing what is going on within you, naming it and making requests around it, the more easily it translates to noticing what is going on with the other person or in the Space Between.

Cultivating Attention

Sometimes, it might be difficult to slow things down in the ways we have described above. The situation may demand that you move faster than you are able to while still offering a high quality of attention.

The good news is that you have been practicing the remedy to this in each chapter in the section "Relationship as Practice", by paying attention, being astonished, and telling someone about it. We each cultivate attention by repeatedly noticing things that live outside of our normal range of consciousness. Exercising your ability to bring subtle things to consciousness expands your capacity to offer curious attention, and thus stay in Third Consciousness.

Relationship as Practice

Remember, small steps can result in big changes over time, and paying attention, being astonished, and telling someone about it are great ways to integrate skills you develop in getting to or remaining in Third Consciousness.

1) During an interaction with someone you know, give them curious attention. Did you notice their behavior change when you gave them this quality of attention?

2) Identify a loved-one in your life (e.g. a romantic partner, a close friend or a family member) that is open to trying the "Creating Sacred Space Ritual" with you. Set up a time to practice this ritual (this can even be done on a video call). Notice what you sense (what it feels like) before and after creating Sacred Space. Notice if your conversation in this space was somehow different than the usual catching up on the details of life. Did you feel heard when you shared something important to you?

3) Try slowing things down using the Sacred Space Incognito method. What was the quality of the conversation after you did this? Was it somehow different than your usual interactions with this person?

4) Notice if it impacted the other person. Did you sense their quality of their attention changed? Did they become more vulnerable?

5) Try making a regular practice out of creating Sacred Space using either of the two methods. This can help you anchor to the pacing and spaciousness so you can access it more often in your interactions with others (even when you don't use this ritual). You will find that you listen more deeply to others, you may find that your vulnerability appears more

easily in your conversations, and you may even find that you feel closer to everyone in your life.

10. EPILOGUE

There came a time when conflict resolution occurred seamlessly between us, when we were tending to the Space Between us such that what was arising could be felt and named, when we were revealing our inner landscape vulnerably and whole-heartedly. If major ways that we hide ourselves have been revealed, adjustments made and a new way of relating is now embodied, is that the end of what Third Consciousness has to offer? No! It is the starting point for even more magic!

In December 2019, we did an envisioning for the upcoming decade. The first step was to review the past decade and to harvest that for which we were grateful. We were startled by how much there was, oftentimes saying, "Wait! Was that only one year?" And then our jaws dropped to the floor when the following timeframe revealed itself to us. At the end of 2016, we asked our Third the question, "What do you desire from us?" Meenal received the phrase, "To be surprised by you, surprised by me, and surprised by each other." Kris saw an image of us teaching together, which he acknowledged and then quickly dismissed because he didn't see himself as a teacher. In a workshop two months later, he accepted that we were meant to teach and we have been on a rocket ride ever since.

In less than 3 years, we had taught about Third
Consciousness in front of a group of 150 people; had created and
led numerous immersive weekend workshops; were co-leaders
of an international retreat; and had led a 6-week course. We
were spontaneously invited to each of those opportunities. And,
now we were on the cusp of completing a book. None of the
experts would ever tell us that all of that could be done so
quickly. Yet we had, because we were creating from Third
Consciousness, and listening to our Third.

****

We hope that by now you have glimpsed through your own
experience that this book is about manifestation. Yes, you read
that correctly - <u>Manifestation.</u> Popular teachers provide tried-
and-proven paths for individuals to use their minds to experience
what they want most from life. Doing that involves
understanding how you are contributing to the repeating
patterns in your life, so that you can free yourself to connect
with the field of consciousness to draw to you the experience
you most desire to have. Sound familiar? That is how we
structured this book.

Through the lens of Third Consciousness, a simplicity
emerges around relationship. A grounded "just is", into which
you can surrender. In each chapter, we have introduced you to a
different facet of this grounded "just is". Life gets really juicy now
because all of the life force energy that was consumed in
maintaining protection-based behaviors is freed up for
something else – Creativity, Passion, Playfulness, Innovation, and
Productivity.

Every time you shift into Third Consciousness, every time you drop an outdated protection-based behavior and choose one that is aligned with Third Consciousness, the Third has taken you another step along a path back to your essence. Essence encompasses a quality of beingness and doingness that is unique to each person. Have you noticed that when a person you know well leaves the room that something palpable is now missing? In contrast, do you find yourself relying on one friend for a particular type of support and another friend for something different just because of who they each are? Both of these experiences point to that person's essence and that essence by its very nature is different from person to person.

Third Consciousness by its very nature encourages you to fully be you, while allowing others to fully be themselves. It becomes easier to embrace surprises with acceptance and curiosity and quite possibly, delight. We free ourselves as well as the other person to show up in the fullness of who we each are, thereby moving from bracing to embracing. When we can let them out of the cage of our expectations and filters, and love them for who they truly are – regardless of whether they are behaving in a way that we don't like or whether they are spreading kindness and joy – we are truly in Third Consciousness.

Our deepest fear is not that we are inadequate. Our deepest fear is that we are powerful beyond measure. It is our light, not our darkness that most frightens us... We were born to make manifest the glory of God that is within us. It's not just in some of us; it's in everyone. And as we let our own light shine, we unconsciously give other people permission to do the same. As we are liberated from our own fear, our presence automatically liberates others. ~ Marianne Williamson

Come Join Us On The Other Side

For us, what has emerged is a wider, broader, deeper day-to-day experience of Love in all of its forms: appreciation/gratitude, joy, laughter, passion, play, wonder, and recognition of a wholistic context that includes all perspectives. Our interactions are frequently peppered with side-splitting laughter when one of us realizes how comical and futile a previously hidden protection-based behavior is. Oftentimes, we will exaggerate soap-opera style the meanings our ever-inventive thinking-minds have created. At other times, we experience a deep level of appreciation for the other person or the situation, through the lens of a bigger context that seems mystical and perfect. We are able to recognize a wholistic truth of what was really going on underneath a pattern that was playing out and how it was emerging to wake us up, despite the pain we experienced through its occurrence. We are living from a deep trust that life is happening for us, instead of to us.

As Kris describes it, "I used to be a tightly-wound person – a literal 'tight-ass'. How I showed up in the world was competent, well-put-together, serious and weighty. This helped me be successful in business, but it came with the price of not truly enjoying life. Instead, I was always trying to control it. I was always bracing to manage the unknown and unexpected. Now I embrace and enjoy how life and people often surprise me."

Meenal shares how rich and nuanced relationship has become, "Recently, I had a mystical ecstatic experience while observing a group interaction. One person said something that two others took in negatively, despite the speaker's intention. In the seconds that it took for the back-and-forth communication to occur, my vision expanded. I could see the two listeners' respective filters and the reason they each reacted the way they did. I could also see the speaker's residue through which the statement was made. Underlying it all, I could see the deeper context for the exchange - the Third was calling the whole group into a deeper relationship via the speaker. I always knew that Third Consciousness was the field of possibilities, but I never guessed I would be able to actually see so many dimensions of relationship at once!"

The Power of Community

One startling and profound realization that we received by listening to the Third is how community is necessary. For years, our practice of listening to the Third felt like a practice between two people in romantic relationship. Community translated into a once-a-month gathering to be witnessed by a circle of couples. 'Relationship as a spiritual path' was something that each couple chose as their practice.

Then, the deeper reality emerged. Relationship isn't simply a chosen path. Relationship is the given path - it is needed. Relationship is the very foundation from which we get to be Love, share Love, and serve Love. In the absence of relationship and community, any of us would spin in circles within ourselves, blindly attempting to navigate the maze of our filters, living out the resulting fun-house-mirror distortions as if they were true. Worse yet, what we project onto other people reflects what we are silently directing inwardly towards ourselves. It is easy to miss the fact that something bright peeks out through the loud self-critical thoughts, meanings, and emotions. Meenal's eyes fill with tears of gratitude at the realization that essence by its very nature is so bright that it invariably shines through, despite her self-critical loop. In the moments when she has lost sight of her essence, she has called upon community to reorient her back towards her essence because they can see what she is unable to see in that moment. The only work she needs to do is to soften in order to receive their offering. We need community in order to discern our self-created distortions from essence.

Community through its diversity helps us grow. Through conflict, we discover the nature of our barriers. We get to see via the other person's differing emotions, words or behaviors, that we are only seeing a slice of reality. Reconciliation with the Third via forgiveness, softens the edges of the filter. Thus, community is integral to developing a broader perspective and an opportunity to better see into which areas we may still need to grow. Broader perspectives are the realm of the Third, so relationship in Third Consciousness is the path forward.

> *You may be able to go faster by yourself, but you can go farther in community. ~ Unknown*

Our Dreams

We dream of a world where groups of people set aside outdated protection-based behaviors, with the visceral recognition that something has to change. We dream of a world where the bigotry of "If you love me, then you'll think and behave the way that I do" is tossed aside in favor of diversity, where essence reigns, where I surrender to your natural strengths as you surrender to mine. We dream of a world where these groups come together to create a stronger relational field, where coherence is the starting point, rather than where we aim to be. From there, the possibilities of what they can do, with each other, for each other, for the planet are limitless. Because we aren't meant to do this on our own. We are meant to do it together.

Appreciation and Gratitude

We hope that you are already using this book to redefine your paradigm for relationship so you too can experience more joy, passion and play in your relationships and your life. We deeply appreciate your trust in the us to take you through this exploration of Third Consciousness. We have been living this work for nearly 15 years and it gives us great pleasure and joy to offer some of the lessons we have learned by listening to the Third. In writing each chapter, we found that there were many things that we needed to omit because there wasn't space to cover them in a digestible way. This required us to get really clear about what we were offering in this book and what we needed to save for other books and workshops. In addition to in-person workshops that we have been offering, we envision using the internet to offer deeper dives into the concepts and practices in this book. As we develop these, you can access them here: http://www.sparkingrelationship.com/rr-one

Thank you for your patience as we continue to explore new ways to offer lessons we have received from the Third.

With Gratitude,
Kris and Meenal

ABOUT THE AUTHORS

We are Kris and Meenal Kelkar. Over the last 30 years we have cultivated the art of relationship. Our focus in this area is on

teaching people about what we call Third Consciousness and the subtle energetics in every relationship. These subtle energies often create patterns, where possible outcomes can be frequent arguments, critical thoughts, repeated complaints, a feeling of walking on egg-shells around each other, and in romantic relationships, lack of physical attraction towards each other, not having sex, or simply a numb feeling of wanting more from your relationship. Since the source of what is going on is in the subtle realm, we are all invited to listen and feel more deeply. Hidden in this subtle realm are magical doorways into the field of amazing possibilities of what relationship can be – this is Third Consciousness. We help people to see and clear the barriers that keep them from what is truly possible in relationship, so they can explore this mystical landscape themselves and with community.

Our coaching and teaching are informed by diverse and cutting-edge consciousness practices, relationship paradigms, and energy work, including Breathwork, Non-Violent Communication, Council, Conscious Loving, Ecstatic Movement, Mama Gena, Joe Dispenza, Tantra, HeartMath, Orgasmic Meditation and various types of energy-healing modalities.

Meenal is a contributing author in the books *"Speaking Your Truth: Courageous Stories from Inspiring Women"* and *"Empowered Voices: True Stories by Awakened Women"*. Kris is the author of *"Dancing with The Field: Bringing Joy, Passion and Play into Everyday Life"*, a widely read book about becoming a creator in life.

http://www.sparkingrelationship.com

Made in the USA
Monee, IL
13 February 2020

21757574R00063